SOME DAY
YOU'LL THANK ME
FOR THIS

The Official Southern Ladies'
Guide to Being a "Perfect" Mother

SOME DAY YOU'LL THANK ME FOR THIS

*The Official Southern Ladies'
Guide to Being a "Perfect" Mother*

GAYDEN METCALFE

AND

CHARLOTTE HAYS

HYPERION

NEW YORK

Library of Congress Cataloging-in-Publication Data

Metcalfe, Gayden.
Someday you'll thank me for this : the official southern ladies' guide
to being a perfect mother / by Gayden Metcalfe and Charlotte Hays.
p.   cm.
ISBN 978-1-4013-0296-2
1. Mothers—Southern States. 2. Grandmothers—Southern States.
I. Hays, Charlotte. II. Title.
HQ759.M48 2009
306.874'30975—dc22
2008055288

Hyperion books are available for special promotions and premiums.
For details contact the HarperCollins Special
Markets Department in the New York office
at 212-207-7528, fax 212-207-7222,
or email spsales@harpercollins.com.

Design by Jo Anne Metsch

FIRST EDITION

10 9 8 7 6 5 4 3 2

THIS LABEL APPLIES TO TEXT STOCK

FOR OUR CHILDREN AND
GODCHILDREN

Gayden Bishop Metcalfe
Harley Metcalfe IV
Kate Bennett
Zephyr Hardy
Zoe Miles
Alston Shackelford

CONTENTS

Contents

ACKNOWLEDGMENTS

THEY ALWAYS SAID that some day we'd thank them, and we do—every day. Just for starters, we wouldn't have had the material for our books without Ann Gayden Call and Julia Morgan Hall Hays, our wonderful Southern mothers. We miss them every day, and, whenever we think we might be turning into them, we thank our lucky stars. Both were great Delta conversationalists, and both gave the lie to William Butler Yeats' contention that souls are had only by those who are "not entirely beautiful." They were belles of every ball and quietly courageous—*and* they knew all the gossip. (P.S. We never sit on strange commode seats or say s-t-i-n-k.)

We can't thank our agent Gail Ross enough—without Gail what we have come to jokingly refer to as our "pastel trilogy" (our three "Southern lady books" have pastel covers) would not exist. Gail shaped and sold the idea and has supported us throughout the process.

We have also been fortunate to work with a great team at Hyperion. We especially thank Leslie Wells for her deft touch with prose and because, a Virginian transplanted to New York, she still speaks Southernese—what more could we ask? Well, one more thing you get in Leslie is an editor who is considerate of authors and gets back to you so quickly you think she's able by some mystical means to read your copy almost before you've hit the "send" button. Anybody who writes for a living knows how much this means.

We are indebted to a host of friends and relatives who shared stories about their mothers and allowed us to use their treasured recipes; we must also thank Gayden's witty nephew Hugh Dickson Gayden Miller for essential help with the sidebars.

We originally considered making a list of great Southern mothers we have known, mothers of our friends, mostly, but we realized this was too fraught with peril—we inevitably would leave out somebody whose charm and kindness has nourished us. So let us just say a general thanks to Southern mothers we have known.

SOME DAY
YOU'LL THANK ME
FOR THIS

The Official Southern Ladies'
Guide to Being a "Perfect" Mother

❧

CHAPTER I

The Southern Mother's Rules for Life

YOU MIGHT BE A SOUTHERN MOTHER IF:

YOU TOOK the initiative to help pick your daughter's husband, silver pattern, nanny, honeymoon destination, and even the flowers in the table decorations—at her birth.

YOU KNOW the route and schedule of every soccer/ballet/fencing/karate mom in the PTA.

Continued

YOU THINK "cheerleading" is an honorable major for your daughter at the University of Mississippi, though you feel a double major in M.R.S. is best.

YOU HAVE an enormous library of small-format videotapes documenting your child's every move since your first sonogram. (If you are a Southern grandmother, you worry that Precious will see the sonogram picture and figure out that it wasn't the stork that brought the baby.)

YOU KNOW the proper technique for hanging and dressing venison.

YOU ACTUALLY shot the deer yourself.

YOU HAVE helped your daughter cram for the all-important exam for her M.R.S. degree. Some people call their exams "finals." The M.R.S.-seeking student calls them "vows."

YOUR HUNTING dogs have better manners than your children (and cost a lot more, too).

Continued

YOU PARTICIPATE in a county-wide exchange program for domestic help when holidays and birthdays come around.

YOU STRAIGHTEN up the house prior to your housekeeper's arrival for fear she will quit if she sees how things really get some days.

YOUR CELL number is on your daughter's teachers' speed dial.

YOU BELIEVE it's better to get an A in deportment than in French.

YOU KEEP a discreet stash of sedatives for the days when report cards come home.

YOU HAVE made *generous* donations to the alumni association at your school to ensure your daughter's acceptance.

YOU RUN into a friend and the first words out of your mouth are "How's yo mo-thuh?"

Continued

(Hugh Dickson Gayden Miller, a Southern nephew, who is also the son of a Southern mother, compiled this list.)

Southern society is arranged along matriarchal lines. The Southern matriarch is a far more formidable creature than the much nicer Southern male. She has to be this way. She has no choice. She was put on earth with a sacred mission: to drum good manners and the proper religion—ancestor worship—into the next generation. Whenever a Southerner sees a man seated while ladies remain standing, she thinks: "I know what kind of mama he had." Mama is well aware that, should she fail, total strangers will someday condemn her with these very words. She reminds us of this frequently.

While Daddy can spoil and dote on his precious little baby dahlin—whom he will still call Precious Baby Girl long after she qualifies for Social Security—it is Mother's duty to turn Precious into a lady and Trey (for the third—Southern mothers love Roman numerals after a son's name!) into a gentleman. The words "lady" and "gentleman" do not connote mere gender to the Southerner. They do not mean "male and female, He created them"; they mean "lady and gentleman, *She* created them." The words "lady" and "gentleman" enshrine a chivalric ideal which Mother must uphold and preserve, even if it kills her, and us. Look on the bright side: This ensures a future income for members of the mental health profession. To achieve her ends, the Southern mother practices shock-and-awe parenthood. She is shocking in her demands and awesome in her subtlety. She speaks in code—the nice code. In the hands of a practiced Southern mother, being nice is lethal; her children and associates often feel that they are being stoned to death by bonbons.

Machiavelli could have taken lessons from the Southern mother. She has perfected the art of diplomatic double-speak. "Aren't you chilly tonight?" is not Mo-thuh's update from the Weather Channel. What she really means: "You look like a floozy. Go upstairs and change right this very minute." If a Northern mother says, "My, it's humid tonight," what she is trying to say is: "My, it's humid tonight." When the Southern mother makes this seemingly innocent statement, what she means is: "Haven't you ever heard of cream rinse? Your hair's frizzier than a grizzly bear's." Beware of the Southern mother who purrs, "It's a beautiful afternoon—don't you want to take a walk?" Translation: "You are fatter than Buddy Boy Jones's 4-H pig." Nor is "You look so pretty with your hair up" as kind as it might sound to the outsider; it actually means: "Get that ugly thicket off your face."

When a Southern daughter has a hot date, Mother will likely present her cheek for a farewell peck. This is not because Mother is starved for affection—she is testing for halitosis.

We have a friend who was not blessed with a Southern mother. But she acquired a Southern mother-in-law. She should have gone to Southern Berlitz school before joining the family. When she and her mother-in-law went shopping together, she was actually pleased whenever Mrs. Nelson Senior said, "That's right cute." We finally had to break the news: If there's anything "that's right cute" *doesn't* mean it's "that's right cute." We explained that neither "right" nor "cute" was the operative word. What Mrs. Nelson was actually seeking to convey was: "That outfit makes you look like the side of a barn, if not the whole damned barn."

The life of a Southern mother is bound by rules, which she in turn uses to make her daughter polite but neurotic. We were going to allow the daughters of our friends to write chapters of this book, but when they started demanding equal time for their therapists, we thought better of the plan. The Southerner, incidentally, is ambivalent about shrinks. Many of us are stark raving mad, or at least crazier than a Betsy bug, though it's hard to differentiate us from all our wacko relatives. Even if Aunt Betty hears voices and prefers dressing in men's clothes, many Southern families will choose to ignore these minor eccentricities. Only vulgar people feel the need to face reality. Nice people pretend Aunt Betty was once in love with a *man*. Emily Potter Aycock had not ventured out of her house for several years when the family doctor cautiously suggested that Mrs. Aycock might benefit from the insights of a gentleman of the psychiatric profession. Her father, Old Man Potter, was insulted. Did the damned fool doctor think a Potter was . . . crazy? Mr. Potter retaliated by paying his dawtah's doctor's bill with bags of nickels. No crazy folks here!

Whenever a support group for DSMs—daughters of Southern mothers—gathers, we almost always discuss Mother's rules. There are heartfelt sighs of recognition. One rule concerns never uttering the word s-t-i-n-k. We know middle-aged DSMs who would rather run nekkid on Main Street than say s-t-i-n-k. Some of these DSMs could take the paint off the side of a barn with their curses. But they won't say s-t-i-n-k. Mother said it wasn't nice. Mother never told us not to use any of the really bad words. She didn't know them. Thank God.

But she did know the rules. Here are the key rules by which a Southern mother lives and which, in her role as preserver of culture, she instills in her daughter, no matter the psychic cost:

1. Never sit on the commode seat in a filling station. Always hover. Hovering is great for the legs. By the way, we say commode, not toilette.
2. Always wear a piece of good jewelry when going to the airport—that way people will know you are from a nice family. (Why do we care? We jes' do. We secretly believe people might treat us nicer if they believe our rich daddy will horsewhip them if they don't.)
3. Speak to all the chaperones. (If you don't, Mother will know because in the Delta there are no secrets.)

4. Don't tell me. I don't want to know.

5. Tell me everything. I am your mother. (We will reveal some of Mother's tricks for pumping the truth out of unsuspecting daughters in subsequent chapters.)

6. Always be nice to the other girls—they'll help you get to the boys.

7. Always wear nice underwear—you may be killed in a car wreck, and you don't want the EMS workers to take one look at your poor dead little body and say, "Well, she certainly wasn't a lady." That would be a fate worse than death.

8. You can date him, but you don't have to marry him.

9. It is as easy to feed a good dog as a bad dog.

10. Never reply to a formal invitation in blue ink.

And the Southern mother's all-time favorite rule of life:

11. Serve left, retrieve right.

The Southern matriarch is bound by genetic makeup to pass along these rules—she cannot help herself; her mother before her did this to her, and her daughters will one day do it to their own daughters. For hundreds of years, no Southern child has been allowed to consume a morsel of food in peace. "Little boats go out to sea," the matriarch will singsong meaningfully if Precious isn't eating bouillon (a favorite matriarch treat) correctly. "I bet the other little girls aren't rude to adults," Mother will say, fully expecting that this will pacify the most recalcitrant three-year-old. The Southern mother believes that on Judgment Day, He will ask: "Did your children stand up whenever an older person entered the room?" She is rarely troubled by theological nuances but sometimes finds herself pondering: Did the twelve Apostles have good table manners? "I'm not sure if God cares if you write thank-you notes with a ballpoint pen," one matriarch confessed in a rare moment of doubt, "but I know I do." "Our children might go to jail," our friend Grace observed, "but it won't be quite as bad if they have nice manners and are sweet to the warden." We are told that this is not a sentiment widely embraced by mothers in other parts of the country.

Another interesting attribute of the Southern mother is that she does not have bodily parts, and she is determined that her daughters won't either—or, at the very least, that we won't know what to call them. "I remember one very clear rule," says Melinda Baskin Hudson, daughter of Greenville's beloved Sally Baskin. "Never refer to your own body part with the same vocabulary that is used for livestock. 'Belly' comes to mind. Goodness, what a common word." It is a miracle that DSMs are able to tell the doctor what hurts.

When Alice Hunt's mother was forced to go to work after her second divorce, she got a job at the House of Fashion, not necessarily the ideal place for a lady who didn't know the names of the parts of the human body. She had, after all, withheld the facts of life from her daughters, through delicacy or ignorance, we aren't sure which. When it came time for her to reveal to her fourteen-year-old daughter that a baby sibling was winging its way to earth, she had not exactly done the groundwork. "Does Henry know?" the perplexed teenager asked. Henry was her stepfather, Mrs. Hunt's then-husband. Mrs. Hunt paused and cleverly pretended to ruminate for a few moments. "Why, yes," she finally said brightly, as if she had just recalled something fascinating, "I believe I *did* mention it to Henry."

Mrs. Hunt came running from a dressing room one day as if she had been shot. But it was worse. She had been hit by something a Southern lady detests far more than speeding bullets (which, truth to tell, she sorta likes): vulgar language. A customer, obviously not the daughter of a nice mother, had used a slang word to describe part of her body. "I refuse to be a part of this," Mrs. Hunt sobbed. She threatened to quit her job, even if starvation loomed. It was several days before we realized she had no idea what the word meant. But she said it sounded bad. By that time, Mrs. Hunt was so thoroughly shocked by her racy new coworkers that wild horses could not have dragged her from the House of Fashion. She also knew that she could hold her head high. She would not have liked to have been called tough. But she was. That is the paradox of the Southern mother: Behind every magnolia façade is a will of steel.

It should be noted that the Southern mother's love of indirect language extends far beyond unmentionable parts of the human body and into all realms of life. "My mother, as were most of our mothers, was a master of the euphemism," recalls Melinda

Hudson. "We don't need to go into that" is the Southern mother's response to any unpleasantness.

Long before the 12-step programs had popularized the concept of denial, the Southern matriarch had elevated it to an art form. Out of sight, out of mind—these are words to live by. The Southern matriarch navigates the shoals of life not seeing anything of which she disapproves. If it is unpleasant, it doesn't exist. Somebody had a ten-pound preemie? Well, isn't modern medicine a marvel! Living in a constant state of denial takes a toll, but it also gives nice Southern ladies a certain vagueness that is useful to their daughters, until they, too, mature and begin to find that it's better just not to know.

We have a friend whose mother, Miss Janie, had a particularly awful experience in New Orleans. Miss Janie felt that it was the proper time to take her two daughters to see the Mardi Gras parades there. On the way to the Rex parade, Miss Janie got caught speeding. The policeman had the gall to insist on taking her in to the police station, where she was fingerprinted, as her daughters gaped in horror at what was not happening. Nice Southern ladies do *not* get taken to the police station (exception: the wild debutante who likes her toddy); though, Miss Janie had to admit, being fingerprinted was sort of fun. All Southern mothers adore being the center of attention, and nothing gets everybody's attention quite like being fingerprinted in a New Orleans jail. On the other hand, being fingerprinted is enough to remind even the vaguest Mississippi lady that she is being held at central lockup. Being arrested is not on any mother's top ten list of genteel things to do. Miss Janie simply pretended it wasn't happening. She faced reality just long enough to call her New Orleans cousin, a lawyer, who came down to the lockup to bail her out. When he said, "I'm here to get my relative out of jail," Miss Janie literally covered her ears. The cousin gallantly told her not to worry about a thing. She didn't.

This turned out to be very bad advice. Summonses from the court in New Orleans began to arrive at her residence in Biloxi. Since Miss Janie did not acknowledge that the unpleasantness in New Orleans had occurred, she stuffed each offensive new summons, soon arriving at an alarming rate, into her sewing basket. "What are you doing with the summonses I bring you, Miss Janie?" the sheriff asked. "Putting them in my sewing box," she replied primly, irritated at the sheriff's effrontery. Finally, the sheriff brought an arrest warrant instead of a summons. Miss Janie was driven downtown in a police car. After her husband arrived and quietly settled the mess, she had to admit her jailbird past, which was the first and last time the events in New Orleans were ever mentioned. From that day forward, Miss Janie never allowed anybody in the family to so much as allude to Mardi Gras or New Orleans. Both had ceased to exist.

We think we know what was going through Miss Janie's mind as Sheriff Akers drove her off in his squad car: "What will the neighbors think?" This is one of Mother's biggest concerns. When the brother of one of our friends became engaged to an overweight redneck, his mother's first thought was, of course:

"What will the neighbors think?" She was also worried that the fat daughter-in-law would ruin a family portrait that was to be done in the spring. This mother has a very Southern mother way of dealing with life's little vicissitudes: She barricades herself in the family's house on the lake until she has worked out a solution, which generally is just a matter of getting her story straight. Usually, the Southern mother just gets out her scissors and snips plump daughters out of family photographs. But that doesn't work so well with oil portraits. Fortunately, Mother was able to come up with a way out of this dicey situation: She persuaded the artist to change the appointment and paint the family a few months early. That way the fat daughter-in-law was not yet a member. The price was obscene—but well worth it.

Another rule by which the Southern matriarch lives: Never learn how to do anything you don't want to do. We know a Leland, Mississippi, grandmother who didn't want to cook or drive—so she didn't learn how to do either of these plebeian tasks. "And Grandmother was never late and didn't starve," her awestruck granddaughter recalls. Our friend Harper's mother loves toodling around town, but she has adamantly refused to learn how to drive in traffic. "Mother doesn't do traffic," Harper explains. This turned out to be important when Harper's mother had to be evacuated from her house because of a hurricane. "We told Mama to get her friends and pack her valuables," Harper recalled. She got her three friends and packed her valuables: the liquor cabinet and casseroles from the freezer. She was going to be somebody's houseguest and she needed to take houseguest gifts (e.g., the casseroles). The liquor cabinet was for herself and her friends. Because of Mother's refusal to do traffic, she eschewed the highway, preferring to drive exclusively on pig trails in Texas. (We think of Texans as Southerners who won their war for independence—and have more money than we do.) It made for a circuitous route. Mother also didn't do gas pumping. When the tank was low, Mother and her immaculately coiffed friends would find their way to a small-town gas station and get out of the car to stand near the pump. "What Galahad might come along and fill our gas tank?" Eventually a stranger would fill the tank and do the credit card for them. Identity theft was never a problem—the Galahad always assumed that the ladies were on some retirement residence's Most Wanted List. Sometimes the Galahad cursed under his breath—which didn't matter, because Southern matriarchs refuse to hear bad language. Mother and her friends would then leave town and continue on dirt roads and shortcuts. However, to reach their destination, they eventually needed to cross a four-lane interstate. Because of the evacuation, a nice policeman was there to conduct traffic. "Mother explained to the policeman that if he just stopped traffic, they could get across," Harper said. He refused. But then Mother sweetly explained that her three friends, all little old ladies, might have heart attacks if he didn't. Would he like to have that on his conscience? As horns were honked angrily, the defeated policeman stopped traffic and let them cross.

It took Mother and her friends three-and-a-half hours to

make what is generally a much longer journey. They were to stay with the son of a cousin of a friend of a friend. "I think your guests are here," their host's secretary announced. "Oh, no," he said, "they won't be here for hours." "Well," she said, "I see four little old ladies driving around the town square in circles." They stayed at his house for three days, playing bridge and consuming the contents of the liquor cabinet Mother had so perspicaciously brought. Harper dutifully called each day. "Oh, they can't come to the phone—a bridge game is in progress," she was told the first day. "I'm sorry but they're out having their hair and nails done," she was told the second. The next day they were hosting a cocktail party. After three days, they felt they had to move on because they had run out of houseguest gifts—and liquor.

As Mother's schedule of activities for Day 2 indicates, the Southern matriarch cares intensely about how she looks, even if she happens to be an evacuee. When one Greenville mother emerged from a complicated back operation, a potentially fatal one, she was asked by her sister-in-law, "Can I get you anything?" "A manicure would be nice," she sighed weakly.

Monogramming is an essential element of home- and self-beautification. The Southern mother will monogram anything that doesn't fight back. Sometimes she must force herself to stop before she gets to her toddler's eyelet underpanties. One reason the competition to be a cheerleader is so intense is that cheerleaders get their names on their bloomers—the next best thing to a monogram. "I'm going to embroider rose petals on your panties" is the Southern mother's way of elaborating on one of her most important maxims: Down in front. We know DSMs in middle age who never sit on porch steps but that Mother's ghost doesn't drive serenely past, waving and making her trademark down-in-front motion.

Unlike her counterparts from other parts of the country, the DSM arrives at school with everything needed for the all-matching dorm room: color-coordinated sheets, towels, and bedspread. Mama herself has monogrammed the pillow shams, which contrast strongly with the DYM's (daughter of Yankee mother) Army Navy blanket. "Give the Southern mother a theme, and she runs with it," said a DSM who shudders at the memory of her all-pink dorm room. When the daughter of a Southern mother is exposed to the daughters of mothers from other parts of the country, she is likely to experience culture shock. "Mother," more than one stunned Delta girl has wailed upon settling into her dorm room, "I just don't know what to make of my roommate. She *didn't even bring* a *dust ruffle*." There is one accoutrement the Southern mother neglects: the reading lamp. You can go blind trying to read in a Southern girl's dorm room. Higher education has never been a Southern mother priority—at least not like homecoming maid/queen, Chi Omega, and/or cheerleading. As we have noted elsewhere, the Southern mother's trifecta is cheerleading, sorority, and marriage. Note: Phi Beta Kappa didn't make the list. It's not a *real* sorority.

If a Southern mother comes across her daughter with her

nose in a book, she is likely to say something like "Since you aren't doing anything, why don't you fix me a glass of ice water?" When the Southern daughter puts her book aside to fix the ice water, she will be barraged with instructions. The Southern mother wants her to fix the glass of ice water correctly. "Take one of my crystal tumblers, add about three cubes of ice," she might say helpfully. Beset with such instructions, our friend Dabney erupted. "Mother, I might not be as great a cook as you, but I can damn well make ice water!" "But, Dabney," Mother said, "this is an old family recipe."

For all the hard work of instilling correct values, a Southern mother expects undiluted homage. You must never write "Merry Christmas, To Mama, Love Irma Jane" on a Southern mother's Christmas present. Instead you write, "Merry Christmas to the most wonderful mother in the world, who has sacrificed her entire life every minute of the day for me and who is also the most beautiful mother in Greenville. You are a saint. All my love forever and ever, your devoted daughter, Irma Jane." When archaeologists dig up the Christmas gift tags of Southern families, they are likely to think we were *all* incestuous, and not just Gramps and Granny, who were double first cousins.

Our friend Alice Hunt adored her mother, but when her mother died, Alice had to finish an assignment in New York that delayed her mother's funeral two days. "I'm sure your mother would have wanted you to do this," said an unknowing associate. "Then you don't know my mother," Alice replied. She explained that Mama would want her to throw herself on a funeral pyre, if the Greenville Cemetery had funeral pyres. It would be perfectly all right, of course, if somebody rescued Alice from the licking flames at the very last minute, but Mrs. Hunt would not have minded the gesture. No extravagant show of devotion ever came amiss to a Southern mother.

And yet, as the DSM approaches a certain stage in life, something strange happens. It is different for all of us. For Alice Hunt, who no longer lives among us, it came shortly after she told her shrink, "Ah want to climb on top of the Chrysler Building and shoot everybody who picks up the wrong fork." The shrink, being unfamiliar with the Southern mother, put Alice Hunt on strong meds instead of commending her for her good values. But it may happen less dramatically. A supposedly bohemian DSM finds herself pitching a hissy fit because somebody has used a vulgar word in her presence, or she refuses to rise with Yankee women when a male guest enters a room. For another it may come when she finds herself eyeing the knickknacks at the Cracker Barrel or getting into inane conversations with total strangers—just like Mama did. For many, it comes when they find themselves telling their own daughters that God will punish them if they don't write their Christmas thank-you notes before New Year's Day.

And then the epiphany strikes:

Mirror, Mirror on the wall,
I am my mother after all.

At some point in her life, every Southern female experiences the shock and awe of recognition: I have turned into . . . her. I AM MY MOTHER.

Her rules are my rules.

I will enforce them, or die trying.

Herb Garden Cucumber Sandwiches

*G*ayden's mother, Ann Gayden Call, one of our favorite matriarchs, died while we were working on this book. As is the old Southern custom, Ann was brought home after her death, and the casket was covered with a beautiful pall. During a brief, at-home communion service, with a lovely Delta breeze blowing through the living room, we heard the Metcalfe dogs, penned for the occasion, bark as if on cue. Their barking ended with the last blessing. All the assembled had one thought: Ann Call would have loved it.

Famously a soft touch at the local humane shelter, Ann Call was so devoted to animals that she did not bat an eye when Gayden's monkey, the aptly named Troubles, threw the contents of the aquarium on the floor. Monkeys will be monkeys, Ann reasoned. Ann's last dog was Mopsy, a lucky animal shelter alumna. Mopsy had Mamie Eisenhower bangs and grew quite obese on Mrs. Call's cooking. Mopsy was an absurd creature, but Ann Call loved her dearly. Mopsy predeceased her mistress by a few months. Gayden was at the airport in Amsterdam when she got the bad news, which she did not want her mother to receive while she was out of the country. Gayden gave directions on her cell phone: "Just wrap her in a nice white sheet, bury her in the country, and don't tell Mama." Stunned passengers quickly moved away from the American Mafiosa with the lilting Southern accent!

We picked this recipe for Ann Call because (like most Southern ladies) she loved a good cucumber sandwich. As they come to fear breaking a hip, older Southern ladies often make a drink and get in bed, where they sip hard liquor and nibble on tiny, crustless sandwiches.

This version of the cucumber sandwich comes from the author Jessica Bemis Ward. Jessica is a kindred spirit because, like us, she has written a book about Southern funeral fare, *Food to Die For.* As our book celebrates the old Greenville Cemetery, Jessica's celebrates the Old Lynchburg Cemetery in Lynchburg, Virginia. She was given this recipe by her friend Mary Jane Hobbs, who in turn found the original rendition in the *Very Virginia* cookbook. She adjusted the recipe, and the result is delicious. It has been acclaimed as the "most eaten" funeral offering at St. John's Church in Lynchburg. Ann Call would approve of our nibbling on Herb Garden Cucumber Sandwiches while toasting her virtues.

*   *   *

SPREAD

Ingredients
1 cup mayonnaise, homemade
1 tablespoon cider vinegar
¼ teaspoon salt
¼ teaspoon paprika
1 tablespoon fresh chopped parsley or 1 teaspoon dried parsley
1 tablespoon fresh chopped oregano or 1 teaspoon dried
1 tablespoon fresh chopped basil or 1 teaspoon dried
1 tablespoon thyme or 1 teaspoon dried
1 tablespoon fresh chopped dill or 1 teaspoon dried
1 tablespoon chopped chives or 1 teaspoon dried
1 tablespoon minced green onions
⅛ teaspoon garlic salt
½ teaspoon Lea & Perrins Worcestershire Sauce
¼ teaspoon curry powder

Combine the ingredients, mixing well, cover, and refrigerate overnight. Spread the mixture on bread rounds and top each with a cucumber slice. Garnish with fresh dill or parsley.

Makes forty to fifty sandwiches.

Mrs. George Archer's Fudge Cake

*O*pen-faced cucumber sandwiches were also a staple of the Coke parties our mothers used to give for us, viewing such paw-ties as a way to preserve civilization. Ethel Archer Davis, who now lives in Corinth, Mississippi, had the most quintessential gatherings. We all wore dresses, and the food was on the dining room table—we ate on the sunporch. We had real plates, real napkins (tea napkins). In addition to the cucumber sandwiches, Ethel always had open-faced tomato sandwiches (as with the cucumber sandwiches, a cookie cutter was used to give the sandwiches a fringe of bread like a monk's tonsure for the upper slice; there was a sprig of parsley in the middle); pimiento cheese sandwiches and chicken salad or tuna fish sandwiches (small with the crust removed); and Ethel's mother's delicious fudge cake. Only homemade mayonnaise was used. Often there was no special occasion—just a get-together. At some Coke parties, we had special crocheted covers for our Cokes. Ethel was kind enough to share her mother's recipe with us.

Ingredients
1 cup chopped pecans
1 cup plain flour
Pinch of salt
2 cups sugar
1 stick butter or margarine
2 squares Baker's Unsweetened chocolate
4 eggs
1 teaspoon vanilla

Chop the nuts onto a piece of waxed paper. Add the flour and salt and mix ingredients with your hands. Add the sugar and mix again. Melt the butter and chocolate in the top of a double boiler. In a large bowl, beat the eggs slightly with a large spoon. Add the dry ingredients and stir. Add the chocolate mixture and stir. Add the vanilla and stir. Pour mixture into a greased 9-inch square cake pan.

Bake in a preheated oven at 350° for 30 to 35 minutes.

Cut into squares and remove from the pan while fudge cake is still warm. It will be soft, so pat into squares and let them cool upside down until they firm up.

Ethel's Homemade Mayonnaise

We can't write a recipe book without homemade mayonnaise. "This recipe sounds so simple," says Ethel, "but for some unknown reason, the mayonnaise sometimes just refuses to make. It could be the mixer speed, the age of the eggs, or the weather— who knows! Don't get discouraged and just try again later. It will be worth the effort."

. . .

Ingredients
2 egg yolks
1/2 teaspoon salt
1 pint Wesson Oil, chilled
Juice from 1 1/2 lemons

Set mixer at low speed. Beat the egg yolks well. Add the salt. Add the oil very, very slowly at a steady pace. When the mixture becomes mayonnaise, add the lemon juice a little at a time. Store in the icebox (more recently known as the refrigerator!).

Blonde Brownies

*M*argie Rosella Kellum, who now lives in Jackson, Mississippi, was one of Greenville's most popular mothers. "Mother made this when we were teenagers and couldn't eat chocolate," her daughter Margaret Roberson of Memphis recalls.

.   .   .

Ingredients
1 stick butter
1 cup sugar
1 cup flour
2 eggs
1/2 cup chopped nuts
1/2 teaspoon vanilla or lemon extract

Soften butter, blend in sugar and flour, add eggs one at a time, and fold in nuts. Pour into 8-inch greased square cake pan. Bake 30 minutes at 350°.

Makes a dozen, but recipe can be doubled.

Vanity Cake

*J*his is an old Southern favorite. Perhaps it's called Vanity Cake because every Southern lady was vain about her own twist. Ann Call would put fig preserves between the layers. Evelyn Hall, her great friend and Charlotte's aunt, used lemon curd. Ann Call didn't "do" icing, and so she always used whipped cream flavored with powdered sugar, vanilla, and a little bourbon or rum. Evelyn might have used her famous seven-minute icing. The style now is not to ice. But the cake is enhanced by a sprinkling of powdered sugar, and you can use a doily for an attractive design. This version appeared in *Recipes Tried and True,* published in 1894.

. . .

Ingredients

1½ cups sugar

½ cup butter

½ cup sweet milk (the old-fashioned term for regular, whole milk)

1½ cups flour

½ cup cornstarch

1 teaspoon baking powder

Whites of 6 eggs

Combine the ingredients and bake in 2 pans in a preheated oven at 350°, putting a frosting of your choice on the top and between the layers afterward. Some cooks like to grate coconut over the finished cake.

Serves twelve.

Fig Ice Cream

*T*his recipe is also proffered in honor of Ann Call, who loved figs in any concoction. This is the "daw-tah's" version, which uses the ice cream machine instead of doing it by hand.

. . .

Ingredients
3 eggs
²/₃ cup sugar
2 cups skim milk
Pinch of salt
2 teaspoons vanilla extract
1 tablespoon lemon juice, fresh not bottled
1 pint figs, chopped, not peeled
1 cup buttermilk

Beat the eggs and sugar together. Add the milk. Cook until the mixture thickens (but not too thick), stirring constantly. Remove from heat and cool. Add a pinch of salt and the vanilla. Mix the lemon juice with the chopped figs. Add the buttermilk and then the chopped figs to the cooled custard. Refrigerate until the mixture is cold. This makes for a better textured ice cream when using La Glaciere, an ice cream maker by Krups. Mrs. Call called this "new-fangled," but it's much easier than an old-fashioned hand-cranked ice cream machine.

This is good served with a fig cake. It's nice to make this ice cream in July when the figs are at their best. This also goes for the cake.

Serves up to ten.

Mrs. Cheney's Fig Cake

When Reynolds S. Cheney II, a beloved former rector of St. James' Episcopal Church, now retired from Holy Communion in Memphis, Tennessee, was first married, his mother, the redoubtable Winifred Cheney, came to visit. Any troubles you'd like me to pray about? the senior Mrs. Cheney asked her son's bride, the late Allan Cheney. No, the newlywed replied, all's fine.

Mrs. Cheney persisted . . . and persisted. Finally Allan admitted that, yes, there *was* a problem: Reynolds looks in the mirror while he brushes his teeth and gets toothpaste all over the bathroom. She assumed that was the end of the matter. A few months later, however, Allan returned from a trip to Jackson, Mississippi, home of her mother-in-law, eyes flashing: It seems that Winifred Cheney had the Daughters of the King, a prayer group inevitably composed of the stodgiest old ladies in any Episcopal parish, praying over Reynolds's and Allan's "trouble in the bathroom." The Daughters had never been so titillated. Allan was less pleased.

In addition to being a "prayer warrior" (Reynolds's term), Winifred Cheney created a wonderful cookbook that, now out of print, is prized by those lucky enough to have a copy. This is Mrs. Cheney's recipe for "a light and luscious cake with the subtle and delicate flavor of the Celeste fig. This would make a fitting dessert for Thanksgiving or other holiday dinners."

.   .   .

Ingredients
1 cup whole fig preserves
2 cups all-purpose flour, measured after sifting
1½ cups sugar
1 teaspoon baking soda
1 teaspoon ground cinnamon
1 teaspoon freshly ground nutmeg
½ teaspoon ground cloves
1 teaspoon salt
1 cup buttery vegetable oil
3 large eggs, room temperature
1 tablespoon vanilla extract
1 cup buttermilk

Remove the stems of the figs and cut each fig into four pieces.

Sift the dry ingredients into a large bowl; blend well with a spoon.

Add the oil, eggs, and vanilla. Beat for 2 to 3 minutes at the medium speed of an electric mixer.

Add the buttermilk and figs and beat 2 minutes more on the same speed.

Pour the batter into an ungreased 13 × 9 × 2 inch pan.

Bake in a preheated 325° oven for 45 minutes or until the cake tests done.

Place on a wire rack while you prepare the topping to pour over the hot cake.

TOPPING

Ingredients
1 cup margarine
1 cup buttermilk
2 cups sugar
2 tablespoons Karo light corn syrup
1 teaspoon baking soda
2 tablespoons vanilla extract

Combine all ingredients except the vanilla and bring to a boil over medium heat in a large and deep saucepan. Boil for three minutes and then add the vanilla.

Pour over the cake enough of the hot sauce, about ¼ of it, to cover the top of the cake.

Serve the cake warm and cover each slice with more sauce.

For best results, allow the cake to remain in the pan and serve from the pan (in the kitchen).

Makes approximately twenty four servings.

Georgia Belle's Three Way Sandwiches

 $\mathcal{G}$ eorgia Belle Cottingham was a pillar of St. James, and the Cottinghams always had a picnic at their house on Lake Ferguson to celebrate St. James' feast day. These sandwiches would be a nice addition to any Coke party. You're going to be shocked by the combination of ingredients—but we guarantee they are delicious.

Here is how Georgia Belle made her three way sand-wiches:

·   ·   ·

Alternate slices of whole wheat and white bread (crust re-moved!). Spread both top and bottom with lots of delicious homemade mayonnaise. Spread homemade pimiento cheese in a thin layer. Spread 1 can of anchovies, mashed with oil from the can (use ¼ of this mixture) in a thin layer. Spread another thin layer of crunchy peanut butter. Chill before cutting off the crusts.

Each sandwich makes eight pieces.

Oysters Anchovy

W hy are Southerners obsessed with anchovies? Our two favorite restaurants, Does' Eat Place and Lillo's, both make salads with generous helpings of anchovies. Ann Call had had several recipes for anchovy dishes, including this one. She noted in her beautiful hand that this was served at Gayden's debutante cocktail supper December 20, 1967. In Mrs. Call's own words, as left behind in her recipe book:

*   *   *

Cut 1½ pounds good sharp American cheese into small pieces. In a skillet heat to a sizzling point a piece of butter about the size of an egg. Add 3 pounds of fresh oysters. Let them cook until their edges curl. Strain the oysters and measure juices.

Add to the juice enough milk to make 6 cups in all and heat this liquid. In a saucepan in the top of a double boiler, melt 5 tablespoons butter or margarine and blend into it 6 tablespoons flour. Remove from heat and add liquid, stirring constantly. Open four 2 ounce cans fillet of anchovy—leaving anchovies in the can, strain off the liquid. Let some cold water trickle gently in can and strain that off (be careful or your anchovies will go down the drain). Mash the fillets with a fork—add with cheese to the hot milk mixture.

Now cook over direct heat or in double boiler until cheese has melted and the sauce is thick and creamy. Double boiler is best but direct heat is fine if you do not forget to stir almost constantly, and it is much quicker.

Add oysters—let them cook a little—if they are going to give off more juice this is the time we want it. Blend 1 tablespoon of cornstarch with ½ cup of milk—add a little of this at a time until the sauce is thick enough to be spooned onto a piece of Melba toast. You may or may not need to add the cornstarch, but if you do, use it all. If the sauce seems a little thick, add a few tablespoons of milk until the right consistency is reached.

Add several good dashes of Tabasco—taste, add more if needed.

Oysters Anchovy can be made hours ahead of time and re-heated before serving. If there is any left after the party bake it next day in scallop shells or a casserole with a thick coating of bread crumbs on top.

Creole Eggs

*D*uring our lifetimes, we've been through everything from "Eggs are good for you. An egg a day will keep the doctor away" to "Eggs will kill you." Now eggs are good for you again. But we have never stopped eating eggs for any reason at any time down here. Southerners love eggs, whether scrambled, poached, or fried (men like them fried) for breakfast or scrambled for a light Sunday supper. We think it's that delicious cholesterol that makes them so good. This recipe has been adapted from one that originally appeared in *Gourmet of the Delta,* published by the women's auxiliaries of St. John's Church in Leland, Mississippi, and St. Paul's in Hollandale, Mississippi, in 1958, and still considered indispensable by the best Delta cooks.

·   ·   ·

Ingredients
1 large onion, chopped
1 green pepper, chopped
1/2 cup chopped celery
Bacon fat
1 can (about 2 to 2 1/2 cups) tomatoes
1 1/2 tablespoons chili powder

Salt and freshly ground pepper to taste
1 cup thick white sauce
Tabasco
12 hard-boiled eggs
Butter
Toasted bread crumbs

Cook the onions, green pepper, and celery in a skillet with bacon fat until soft. Add the tomatoes, chili powder, salt, and pepper. Cook until thick. Combine with the white sauce. Season well, using more salt, pepper, and Tabasco. Slice the eggs in round slices and place in a lightly buttered casserole, alternating a layer of sauce with a layer of eggs. Repeat until all is used. Top with buttered crumbs. Bake at 350° for 30 minutes or until hot and bubbly. This freezes well. Shrimp may be added for a nice luncheon dish.

Serves ten.

Foolproof Soufflé
(from a non-cook)

$\mathcal{T}$his is an old recipe that came from the recipe book of Florence Metcalfe, Gayden's husband Harley's mother, written just as she recorded it. Mrs. Metcalfe might not have been a cook, but she surely could write. Her hand was beautiful. All her recipes were written on the backs of greeting cards or stationery with the name of the "owner" of the recipe at the top. We can attest that this is delicious—and a good, easy recipe for Mrs. Metcalfe's fellow non-cooks. It also contains one of Delta cuisine's essential ingredients: cream of mushroom soup.

• • •

Ingredients
4 ounces sharp Cheddar cheese
1 can undiluted cream of mushroom soup
4 eggs, separated
Salt and freshly ground pepper to taste

Grate the cheese and combine it with the mushroom soup in a saucepan. Over moderate heat, stir until the cheese has melted. Set aside to cool.

When it's cooled, stir in the the egg yolks and mix thoroughly.

Meanwhile, beat the egg whites in a soufflé dish until fairly stiff.

Now stir in the soup and cheese mixture, folding together gently so the egg whites don't break down. Add salt and pepper to taste. Cook 30 minutes in a preheated 350° oven.

Serve. You can't miss!

Serves six.

Jennie Lake's Peach Pickles

*J*ennie Lake was a dear friend of Mrs. Metcalfe's. As long as we're plundering the matriarchal recipe books, we can't resist sharing Mrs. Lake's peach pickles. There is only one thing more exciting to Southerners than home-grown tomatoes: peaches. This is a good way to use a peach. It's pickling and doesn't involve canning, a rural art. Pickling is a Delta art, for peaches and people.

.　　　.　　　.

Ingredients
4 quarts peaches
2 pounds sugar
2 cups vinegar
1 1/2-ounce stick of cinnamon
1/4 ounce whole cloves

Dip the peaches quickly in hot water and remove the skins.

Boil the sugar, the vinegar, and the cinnamon for 20 minutes, until it is a syrup. Place peaches (a few at a time) in the syrup and cook them until they are tender. Pack them in clean jars, placing a few cloves in each jar.

Adjust the rubbers and fill each jar to overflowing with the hot syrup.

Screw tops on tight so no air will be present and seal the jars immediately. You do not have to put these in a hot water bath. The longer they sit, the better they get.

Yields approximately four 1-pint jars.

Berkeley's Potato Rolls

Southerners love good rolls. Even the Southern male will carry on a knowing conversation about the quality of homemade rolls. This recipe comes from Berkeley Crittenden Thomson, a Greenville native who, after many years in California, now lives in Jackson, Mississippi. All who have tasted Berkeley's rolls vow that they are the best they've ever put into their mouths.

· · ·

Ingredients
1 fresh yeast cake
1/2 cup lukewarm water
1/2 cup sugar
2 tablespoons salt
2/3 cup Crisco shortening
1 cup mashed potato
1 cup scalding milk
2 eggs, beaten
5 to 6 cups flour
Butter

Put the yeast in the water. Mix the sugar, salt, shortening, and potatoes in a large bowl. Pour the scalding milk over this and let it cool. Add the yeast and water and mix well. Add the beaten eggs. Stir in the flour until stiff and then knead. Put in a large bowl. Grease the top with soft butter. Cover and leave in refrigerator 24 hours.

Take out 2 hours before time to serve and make into rolls. Let them rise. Bake for 15 to 20 minutes at 375°. These rolls will keep one week in the refrigerator—take out as needed.

Baked Tomatoes Robertshaw

The late Sylvia Robertshaw, a beloved Delta mother, who often played the organ at St. James, used to joke about the stress of being married to a great cook. Jimmy Robertshaw was not only a great cook but he was a prominent lawyer. Among Mr. Robertshaw's accomplishments (as a lawyer) was getting the first legal whiskey license in Mississippi for a client . . . not surprising that the store was in Greenville, heart of the Delta and heavy drinking. He was also a duck hunter of renown, and Mrs. Robertshaw served tomatoes with "Jimmy's baked ducks." We remember eating them thirty years ago!

. . .

Ingredients
1 medium onion, chopped
1 large green bell pepper, chopped
3 tablespoons unsalted butter
4 cans (14½ ounce each) tomatoes
  (two Italian seasoned and two plain diced). Do not drain!
3 teaspoons dark brown sugar
2 teaspoons Lea & Perrins Worcestershire Sauce
4 or 5 good dashes Tabasco sauce

¼ teaspoon Tony Chachere's Seasoning
1 cup Pepperidge Farm stuffing mix (comes in a bag)
Salt and freshly ground pepper to taste

OPTIONAL TOPPING
1 cup grated sharp Cheddar cheese

Sauté the onion and green pepper in butter. Add the tomatoes (straight from the can . . . juice and all). Add the balance of ingredients and mix well. Pour into a buttered 3-quart dish. Sprinkle with the cheese and bake in a 350° oven for 30 minutes. Delicious served hot or at room temperature.

Serves eight to ten.

SOME SIGNS YOU MIGHT BE A DSM

You Never Leave Home Without Your Bed Made, Even If You Have to Make It Yourself.

You Play the "Who Do You Know?" Game. Whenever we meet anybody new, it is important to ascertain their social status (without being rude). We do this by

Continued

---

playing the "Who Do You Know?" Game. As with other games, we start high and go low. "Do you know So and So, the president of the bank?" "No? Well, then, how about the . . ." Only you can determine your cutoff point. Mama didn't have to teach us the rules—we imbibed them from her. And, by the way, we aren't fooling anybody.

You Are Obsessed with Silver. We recognize all the major silver patterns at a glance. When a DSM is confronted with a Rorschach test, she doesn't say, "Well, I see a big old grizzly bear coming to eat me up." She says, "Why, yes, I think that's Chantilly." If it is an ornate blot, she will say, "That is definitely Francis I." You wouldn't believe the number of male psychiatrists in Jackson who have taken early retirement after listening, hellish session after hellish session, to a DSM sobbing about who got Aunt Boo Boo's silver tea service.

You Believe Some Undeserving Yankee Family Is Still Using the Silver That Their Ancestors Stole from Ours.

Continued

You Know About Deviled (Stuffed in the Delta) Egg Plates, Pledge Pins, and the Importance of Middle Names.

You Refuse to Stand Up for a Man. Yankee women at a dinner party will sometimes stand when a male guest arrives. It is a painful sight for us. We wish we weren't too polite to tell them how wrong this is. Gentlemen stand for ladies—not the reverse, unless it's Prince Charles or a very elderly man.

You Continue to Stand Up for Older Ladies Long After It Dawns on You That You Are an Older Lady Yourself. You only stop when you realize people are thinking, "What's this grizzled old bat doing giving me her seat? Do I look *that* bad?"

You Speak to Everybody, Even Tacky People. Mama always said part of being a lady is not being a snob—at least not getting caught. Always remember how Melanie treated Belle Watling in *Gone with the Wind.*

Continued

48

You Are Prone to Say, "My Daddy Would Horsewhip You for This," Whenever Your Husband Displeases You.

You Know What Tomato Aspic Is.

You Only Use White Meat to Make Chicken Salad.

You Play Mahjong, but You Prefer Bridge—It's Nicer.

Is it a coincidence that DSM also stands for that other DSM—the famous Diagnostic and Statistical Manual our shrinks use?

CHAPTER II

Grandmothers:
Why Precious Angel Baby Grandchildren
Are So Much More Fun
Than Granny's Own Bad Children

WE REVERE older ladies in the Delta. Quite a few of our sweet old dears are not above taking advantage of this, and grandmothers are the worst offenders. Southern grandmothers don't so much age as they marinate. The older they get, the stronger they become. A Delta dowager can do no wrong, not in our eyes, and certainly not in hers. Nobody is permitted to bat an eye if a sweet old thing pipes up and says something so mean it makes your hair stand on end. This is her prerogative. She is, after all, *an old lady*. In fact, she is fond of reminding us: "*I am an old lady.*" This is the next best thing to having a license to kill in polite Delta society.

Quite often when our sweet old dears say something ugly about another human being, the bon mot is uttered in a stage whisper—actually, the word "stentorian" springs readily to mind—and the unfortunate target of the remark is not spared. We must pretend we didn't hear what Granny said. This happens because aging glamour girls refuse to wear their hearing aids. (An alternative theory: It's just plain fun to say whatever the hell you damned well please, when you've reached the age when you can.) We smile and nod, and hope Granny won't elaborate. But we dare not interrupt her. As an old lady, she has become irreproachable—even if she happens to fall into that not numerically insignificant subset of sweet old dears who are about as sweet as a yard dog on spa food. We know quite a few Southern females, many of our dearest friends among them, who have been storing up mean things to say their entire lives, just waiting for that exhilarating moment when they can utter them with absolute impunity. This moment is known to arrive with the nativity of the first grandchild, after which blessed event nobody dares cross Grandmother. "Don't upset Mama," Southern families say constantly. Of course, Mama is under no obligation not to upset us. And she usually finds a way. It has been speculated that the impressive longevity rate among our old ladies occurs because the precious old dears do anything and everything they please, and are never forced to keep anything bottled up inside them—that's our job.

A Southern grandmother sees her role in life as twofold: undermining Mother's rules, the very rules of which she was once the chief enforcer, and providing refuge against what she sees as Abu Ghraib in the Mississippi Delta. That would be the reign of Mother. "Why is sweet little Meriwether upset?" accusatory Granny asks, while little Meriwether, purple with rage, her eyes flashing like Linda Blair in *The Exorcist,* bangs her sweet little angel head against the banister. Granny wants to know what Mother has done to the poor little thing. Granny is totally uninterested in whatever offense the little innocent has committed. Mother knows when she is defeated. The very mother who made her what she is has now turned against her. Mother eventually has a startling revelation: What gave Granny the will to live all these years was that she planned to enjoy every minute of watching her grandchildren torture her daughter, much the same way she was tortured by Mother. We feel certain that this is a cycle that will be repeated until kingdom come.

Granny, of course, has a nuclear weapon in her arsenal: *I am an old lady.* We belatedly realize that we have been told all our lives that the old are to be honored because Granny was planning to become an old lady. It was a plot, engineered by our own duplicitous mothers. Our only hope is that we, too, will one day be old ladies and, as such, in a position to intrigue against our own daughters, on behalf of our precious grandchildren. Turnabout is fair play, we say, though—like Granny—we have no intention of playing fair when our turn comes.

Grandmother's favorite thing is to egg her grandchildren on

to do things for which she would have killed us. This harmless pastime adds a certain je ne sais quoi to her sweet old life. Tootsie Berry Shackelford, whose real name was Frances before she was promoted to grandmother, made Captain von Trapp in *The Sound of Music,* who summoned his children by blowing a whistle, look like a pushover when it came to instilling table manners. She forced her often recalcitrant offspring to dress like Princess Elizabeth or Little Lord Fauntleroy, who wore ruffled collars, had beautiful manners, and, perhaps more to the point, worshipped his mother. Granny's other models of child dressing were *The Blue Boy,* by Gainsborough, and *The Age of Innocence,* by Sir Joshua Reynolds. You'd be amazed at how many little girls in the Delta have Sir Joshua's niece hanging in their bedrooms. (They probably think she is an ancestress.)

But back to Tootsie Berry: Tootsie Berry loved having her dear little grandchildren gather around, in their finest, all dressed up to visit Granny, and placed around the very formal dining table where her own brood had been instructed in the more excruciating points of etiquette. And what finer point of etiquette did Tootsie Berry instill in her grandchildren on these important occasions? The fine art of pea shooting. "Come on, Sam Wilson! Come on! You can hit the chandelier!" she was heard urging. When Tootsie Berry's grandchildren came to dinner, pea soup meant something other than what you eat in a bowl. "Isn't Tootsie Berry *fun?*" Tootsie Berry was fun when we were growing up, too. We have the happiest of memories of gathering in her bedroom at daybreak—which happens around noon in the

Delta—drinking coffee and talking about the night before. Tootsie Berry was a great raconteur, and we laughed and laughed. However, we would not have laughed and laughed if one of us had dared shoot a pea at Tootsie Berry's fine ceiling. But then we were not precious angel grandchildren who could do no wrong.

Although the Delta abounds in fine cooks, we have to admit that many of our grandmothers' generation weren't so hot. Cooking wasn't the done thing, so to speak. "When my father brought my mother home to meet her future in-laws," recalls our friend Susan Kirk Cook, "my grandfather said, 'Helen, do you know how to cook?' She replied, 'No, sir, I don't.' And he said, 'Don't learn how, and you will never have to.'" Grand-mothers who could barely boil water without burning it when they were mere mothers will try to whip up meals for their grandchildren. The results of these forays into unknown territory—i.e., the kitchen—are mixed at best. When asked for a hamburger by a hungry grandson, one determined Delta grandmother foraged in her daughter's pantry until she located a burger. She fried it in butter and placed it between two buns—it was then that she was politely informed that it was a Gainesburger. Gus, the hunting dog, was called in and he gained about twenty cholesterol points from the butter. These are just two of Greenville's non-cooking grandmothers. One grand-mother did the floor plan for a big new house all by herself. When she ran it by an architect before turning the project over to the contractor, the architect said, "Well, Miz Mitchell, it's a nice house except that you left out a room—the kitchen."

While Granny was never rude to us when we were children—rude is the worst thing you can be in the Delta, better to just murder somebody than be rude—she often laid down the law in no uncertain terms. She does not like for us to lay down the law in no uncertain terms to her precious grandchildren. She suddenly believes that children are rational beings who should never be made to do anything that displeases them. This was not her philosophy when we were growing up. But now she must offer a haven to those innocents oppressed by Mother's unreasonableness. Thus the alliance between Grandmother and her grandchildren forms. Mother says you can't wear a strapless gown to Miss Maud's nursery school? Well, we'll see. Granny volunteers to drive Baby Girl to school the next day so that Mama doesn't know until afternoon that Baby Girl showed up at Miss Maud's looking like a four-year-old tart. Eat your green beans? Not if you don't want to, Precious. Come to Granny's house, and we'll have sweet tea so thick with sugar that it looks like gravy for the Sunday roast. This is after years of starving us into evening dresses. But that was then. Today Granny knows that Mother, who is no fun at all, must be resisted at all costs. Unfortunately for Mother, she is well up to the task.

Pets afford a venue in which Granny is particularly able to thwart Mother. She is ever eager to be of service to grandchildren who yearn for vicious and/or filthy pets. A ferret? Granny says be sure and bathe it in the bathtub instead of outdoors, where it could catch cold and die (which is what Mother secretly hopes will happen). Gayden Bishop Metcalfe didn't want a ferret, however—she had her heart set on a woolly monkey. Big Gayden had had a woolly monkey herself, and knew a thing or two about monkeys. She remembered the sad day Troubles had teamed with his paramour, Merry Christmas, also a woolly monkey, to kill their own children. She did not want any more Troubles. Gayden Bishop, who might have been willing to trade her baby brother for a pet monkey, wailed. Mama was unjust and wrong, she said. Ann Call, her supportive grandmother, agreed. A woolly monkey was, her grandmother felt, a perfectly reasonable request. For a while, Big Gayden wouldn't let the dynamic, monkey-obsessed duo go to Memphis together, for fear they'd come home with a monkey. But they set about outsmarting her. And it might have worked out fine, if only Big Gayden hadn't answered Mrs. Call's phone the day the monkey rescue league called.

"No, thank you," said Big Gayden. "I'm already looking at two monkeys, and they are in big trouble." After not getting their monkey, Ann Call and Gayden Bishop were forced to hole up at Mrs. Call's house, sulking, for days. Mrs. Call never uttered a word against Big Gayden. She didn't have to. "I think her daddy would have let her have it if monkeys knew how to fetch ducks," said Uncle Dickson, who himself has a monkey. (Please, whatever you do, don't call us eccentric down here.)

Nothing is more distressing to a grandmother than Mother's fussing at children. "I was not a mother who fussed—I disciplined," Julia Hays once remarked. It must be noted that hers was not exactly an iron discipline. "Tell me *again* why you are home?" she'd implore each time her daughter made an un-planned, discipline-related trip home from school. She expected this tradition of outer space–based parenting to be carried on to the next generation. When her older daughter, Little Julia, the mother of three squabbling children under four, leaned out the window and shouted, "Cut it out this minute!" Julia Hays thought she was going to faint. That poor little children—who were clobbering each other within an inch of sending each other to the emergency room—should be spoken to like that! Did Granny feel an asthma attack coming on? She silently urged herself to remain calm and offer parenting tips: Instead of rais-ing your voice, she explained, it was better to go outside, kneel down, look the little angels in the eye, and explain, in a soft voice, that it is ill-mannered to hit each other. Yes, that would do the trick. "I know," she said, preening, "I brought up two daughters." She forgot to mention that they were fourteen years apart, which is akin to having one child twice.

Later in the day, when one of the little hyenas needed stitches, Grandmother Julia blamed . . . the parents. That's what comes of raising your voice to your children: The darling hearts be-come flustered and try harder to kill each other. Her bond with her granddaughter was cemented by her oft-repeated adage: "Good skin skips a generation." The elder Julia had had great skin. Another granny-watching tip: If you are the spinster aunt, keep an eye on the jewelry. Granny will want somebody with beautiful skin to have it.

Granny's fondest dream is to have a baby named after her. If there is one thing Granny feels strongly about it's what she calls "names snatched out of thin air." Southern grandmothers are not Jason-oriented. The definition of a bad name: names this family has not previously hallowed. We know a grandmother who offered $5,000 to the first grandchild to name a baby Eugenia, after her. The next grandchild was christened Zelda. Grandmother is not speaking to her traitor daughter, but she has bought Zelda every expensive toy on earth. Wait until Eugenia comes along. . . .

All Southern grandmothers have a circle of vivacious friends, with whom they play bridge, drive around town together like bats out of hell, and enjoy cocktails. One group of Delta grandmothers gathers every Sunday evening for Vespers—or that's what they call it. But it's not at church and it's for cocktails, not evensong. Southern grandmothers like drinks that are dark brown from the high degree of hard liquor. Old ladies love hard liquor. But if a granddaughter is coming for Vespers, they buy a bottle of white wine for her. Not letting girls have strong drink is Granny's way of being protective, sort of like not letting little children drink coffee. Granny may strongly imply that she has only lately begun to go in for the hard stuff, which is a lie.

Granny's bridge and gossip sessions, we must report, can turn cutthroat, as sweet old ladies exercise their famous right to say anything that comes into their dear old heads. "Get me out of here," one stranded granddaughter begged her mother. "I'm drowning in white wine and vicious gossip." It is the only known instance of a granddaughter siding with her mother against

Granny. All in all, Southern granddaughters adore Granny and regard her as an ally in the eternal battle against Mama.

As you are beginning to see, it was our Southern grandmothers who put the *grand* in grandmother. If there is a Southern doctrine of infallibility, it goes like this: Granny is always right, especially when she espouses the cause of her grandchildren. We cannot end without mentioning the Southern grandmother's favored prop: the cane, or stick, as she likes to call it. We have already noted that the vanity of aging glamour girls prevents them from wearing their hearing aids. Vanity does not prevent them from using canes. Quite the contrary. A figural or silver-headed cane is highly desirable. The cane has a number of uses: It drives home the notion that Granny is *an old lady,* and thus entitled to do anything—and absolutely everything—she takes it into her head to do, on account of her (feigned) feebleness. Also, a cane can be brandished for emphasis. This is nice for Granny when she is making a point. All in all, a cane adds grandeur. It's sort of like when Granny is stopped for speeding and she tells the policeman, "Go on, young man, I was driving before you were born."

Southern mothers may be defeated by the unholy alliance of their own mothers and daughters—the only thing that keeps them going is the hope of one day being able to say, "I am an old lady." When this happens, just you wait. We'll show you how to be grand because, after all, we learned from champions. You won't know what hit you, unless you see our canes coming at you. Thank you, Mama, for showing us how much fun old age is going to be.

GRANDMOTHER'S TREATS

Gingerbread with Lemon Sauce

*T*his is a treat grandmothers like to serve their little angels. Gayden remembers having gingerbread on a lovely white dessert plate. The gingerbread was cut into small squares and covered with delicious, tart lemon sauce. Actually, it was floating in a pool of lemon sauce. Ann Call always said, "Eat all you want—ginger is good for you." Well, it has all of one tablespoon of ginger, and God only knows how many calories. But back then, who cared!

. . .

Ingredients
1 cup dark brown sugar
1 cup molasses
1/2 cup warm water
1 stick unsalted butter, cut into pieces
1 1/2 cups Crisco
1 tablespoon powdered ginger
1 teaspoon cinnamon

¹/4 teaspoon ground cloves
¹/2 teaspoon ground nutmeg
2¹/2 cups all-purpose flour
2¹/2 teaspoons baking soda
¹/2 teaspoon salt
2 eggs, beaten

Preheat oven to 350°. In a saucepan combine the sugar, molasses, water, butter, Crisco, and the seasonings. Cook over medium heat until the mixture boils. Remove from heat and allow it to cool. Meanwhile, sift the flour, soda, and salt. Make a well in the dry ingredients and pour in the cooled mixture. Add the beaten eggs and mix until incorporated. Bake in a greased 9×11 dish for 30 minutes or until the edges pull away from the pan. Cool slightly and serve with lemon sauce.

Makes two dozen nicely sized squares.

LEMON SAUCE FOR GINGERBREAD

Ingredients
1 large lemon
¹/3 cup lemon juice
4 eggs
³/4 cup sugar
Pinch of salt
4 tablespoons unsalted butter

Zest the lemon and juice it (removing seeds). Add enough fresh lemon juice, if necessary, to make ⅓ cup. Separate the eggs, saving whites for another use. In the top of a double boiler, mix the 4 yolks, sugar, lemon juice, 1 full tablespoon of lemon zest, and salt.

Cook over simmering water until the mixture has thickened. Remove from heat and stir the butter into the mixture by tablespoons.

After the sauce has cooled, taste for tartness. Add more zest if necessary. This sauce thickens considerably after refrigeration. It can be stored in the refrigerator for up to two weeks.

Makes one cup.

Strawberry Shortcake

*T*here are always sweets at Grandmother's house. Like Mama, Granny wants you to be thin. Unlike Mama, she can't resist feeding you good things. Another reason to visit Granny! Glossary: K-Roger is Delta-ese for Kroger. We're so cute!

. . .

Ingredients
1 to 2 pints fresh strawberries
Confectioners' sugar
1 pint whipping cream
Vanilla flavoring (optional)
Pound cake, often the commercial variety
*   available at the K-Roger*

Wash the strawberries just prior to using. Pat dry. If you wash the berries too soon and allow them to sit, they will get mushy. Remove stems and slice. Add confectioners' sugar to taste. Whip the cream until soft peaks hold. Fold in confectioners' sugar to taste. Add a touch of vanilla flavoring if desired.

Slice the cake, horizontally, into three sections. Using a slotted spoon, cover two sections with strawberries and then stack one on top of the other. Place the third layer on top of that and ice the entire cake with the flavored whipping cream. Allow the cake to "rest" in the icebox, gently covered. Serve after chilled, even better the next day!

Serves six to eight.

Victoria Cake

*T*his is one of our South Carolina friend Linda Weiss's recipes. Linda, the author of several cookbooks, went all the way to Le Cordon Bleu to find out that the techniques she'd learned at home in the South are considered high art. She says that this cake is named after Queen Victoria because she loved teatime. We included it for two reasons: We felt it was appropriate because Queen Victoria was known as the "grandmother of Europe" (due to the fact that so many of Europe's royals were descended from her) and because this cake is delicious. Linda likes to put it on a cake pedestal and cover it with a pretty tea towel. It can be filled with any jam or curd. Linda says that strawberry, raspberry, blackberry, or apricot jam or lemon curd are all excellent fillings. You just have to choose one.

. . .

Ingredients
1 cup unsalted butter, softened
1 cup sugar
4 large eggs, beaten
2 cups self-rising flour

Preheat over to 375°. Spray two 7- or 8-inch pans with baking spray. Cream the butter and sugar with a wooden spoon or mixer until light and fluffy. Add the beaten eggs gradually, making sure the eggs are well mixed into the butter and sugar mixture. Add the flour gradually, mixing thoroughly. Divide the mixture between the pans. Bake for 20 to 25 minutes or until the cake tester comes out clean. Cool for ten minutes in the pan. Remove to a wire rack to cool. Place jam or curd between the layers and sprinkle the top with sugar.

Prune Whip with Custard Sauce

Should you ever trust a recipe that comes from someone who weighs seventy pounds drippin' wet? That was Harley's Aunt Jane, but we must say that this recipe from her collection of recipes—we're not sure Aunt Jane herself actually knew where the kitchen was—is delicious.

.   .   .

Ingredients
1 package (12 ounces) pitted prunes
3 teaspoons lemon juice (fresh, not bottled)
2 egg whites
1/4 cup sugar
1/4 cup heavy cream whipped
Confectioners' sugar to taste

Cook the prunes until soft. Drain and save the liquid. In a food processor, puree the prunes. Add the lemon juice. Beat the egg whites until stiff but not dry. Gradually add the sugar, until stiff peaks form. Fold in the prune puree until well incorporated. Divide among six dessert or fruit coupes and chill. Serve napped with custard sauce. Heavy cream whipped with confectioners' sugar to taste will gild the lily.

CUSTARD SAUCE

Ingredients
1 cup milk
2 egg yolks, beaten
3 tablespoons sugar
Pinch of salt
1 teaspoon vanilla

In the top of a double boiler, warm the milk until near a boil. Combine the well-beaten yolks with the sugar and salt. Add a little of the hot milk and mix. Return this mixture, all the while whisking, to the milk/double boiler.

Cook over hot, not boiling water, until the mixture coats a spoon.

Remove from heat and stir in the vanilla. Cool and refrigerate until cold.

Serves six.

Grasshopper Pie

$\mathcal{T}$ his is Granny's idea of going green—with crème de menthe. This pie is light, alcoholic, and perfect to serve with any type of game. Think holidays, too. Green, you know.

For overkill and those not recently released from rehab: Serve dessert with a glass of crème de menthe and a nut dish (individual, silver of course) holding fried walnuts. From soup to nuts.

. . .

CHOCOLATE CRUST

Ingredients
1½ cups chocolate Oreo cookie crumbs
¼ cup real butter, very soft to melted

Roll the Oreos with a rolling pin until crushed. Add the butter and mix.

Pat into a 9-inch pie plate.

FILLING

Ingredients
23 large marshmallows
1/2 cup whole milk
4 tablespoons crème de menthe
2 tablespoons white crème de cacao
1/2 pint whipping cream, whipped
Shaved sweet chocolate

In the top of a double boiler, over boiling water, melt the marshmallows in the milk.

When this mixture is cool, add the crème de menthe and crème de cacao. Fold in the whipped cream.

Pour into the prepared shell and chill for several hours or overnight. Just before serving, garnish with shaved chocolate.

Serves eight.

The Rosedale Sandwich

G randmothers are great with leftovers. This is one of the best after–Christmas Day lunches we have ever eaten. It's messy but divine. (An excellent recipe for turkey dressing can be found on page 144.) Mrs. Call served pickled peaches as the accompaniment; the ones from the glass jar were acceptable if your naughty friends failed to give you homemade. We don't, by the way, know why this sandwich is named after the Delta town of Rosedale, but we do know you'll like it.

· · ·

Ingredients
Homemade mayonnaise
Sliced turkey
Dressing
Cranberry sauce
Sandwich bread, whole wheat preferred

Assemble as any sandwich and indulge.

Carrot Ring with Petit Pois

S hoot your peas and eat your carrots! Gayden remembers her grandmother sitting with a little pad at her phone dialing 8-3, which was the entire telephone number for Cascio's Grocery in Leland, Mississippi. She would order "petit pois, lemon cookies, and Co-colas." The groceries arrived by bicycle. Le Sueur "petit pois" sound a bit grander than they actually were. These peas are not only delicious but excellent for aiming at Granny's chandelier.

Sometimes Ann Call would drain the juice from a can of Le Sueur tiny peas, rinse them with cold water, and warm them in a little chicken broth with some fresh mint. The best peas came later when she found out about Birds Eye. Whoooo! Then she would sauté the little babies in butter and add a little mint at the end—too good to shoot. The French—whom we didn't know too much about then (it was before Food Network and Julia Child)—cook their peas with lettuce. Or you can puree them, a nice English dish called pease. We call it Gerber.

Ingredients
2 bunches carrots, peeled
1 tablespoon sugar

1 tablespoon minced green onions
¹/₂ cup minced celery
1 tablespoon unsalted butter
2 egg yolks, beaten
Fresh nutmeg
Fresh green peas, enough to fill center after being steamed

Cook the carrots until soft. In a food processor, blend until fairly smooth. Add the sugar. Sauté the onions and celery in the butter until just wilted. Add to the carrot mixture. Fold the yolks into the mixture.

Add a sprinkle of fresh nutmeg. Put the above mixture in a greased ring mold and place in a pan of hot water in a 350° oven.

Bake until set, about 30 minutes. Invert the mold on a serving plate and fill the center with green peas, buttered and seasoned lightly.

Serves six.

Calf's Liver with Mustard Sauce

*A*nother favorite of grandmothers! But this recipe was developed by the late John Currie, who tinkered with a French cookbook.

. . .

Ingredients
4 to 6 slices of calf's liver
Dijon mustard
Salt and freshly ground pepper to taste
Flour
4 tablespoons butter
2 tablespoons vegetable oil
Chopped parsley
Dash of paprika (optional)
Mustard Sauce (recipe follows)

Pat the liver dry and smear with a bit of mustard.

Mix salt and pepper with the flour. Dredge (coating well) each piece of liver (both sides). Melt the butter and oil together in a large frypan. Sauté the liver until it is browned. Be sure that the liver remains a bit pink in the center—don't overcook. A thicker piece of liver prevents the "shoe sole" effect commonly found in liver smothered in onions. Also, use tongs to turn your liver—no piercing . . . difficult for this generation.

Remove the liver to a serving platter, nap with the mustard sauce, and sprinkle with chopped parsley and a dash of paprika (optional).

MUSTARD SAUCE

Prepare earlier and hold.

Ingredients
1/2 cup canned beef consommé
1/2 cup dry white wine
1 cup heavy cream
3 tablespoons unsalted butter
2 tablespoons Dijon mustard
Salt and freshly ground pepper to taste

Combine the consommé and wine in a saucepan and mix gently while heating. When the liquid has been reduced by half, stir in the cream (slowly). After the sauce has thickened, remove from heat and incorporate the butter and mustard. Correct the seasonings if necessary.

Serves four to six.

Potato Soup

*W*e put this in this particular chapter because it is the ultimate comfort food, and grandmothers love to provide comfort—and comfort food—for those darling hearts.

.   .   .

Ingredients
2 large Irish baking potatoes
1 large yellow onion, chopped
2 tablespoons unsalted butter
1 can (28 ounces) diced tomatoes with basil/garlic/oregano
4 cups water
1 teaspoon salt
3/4 teaspoon white pepper
Pinch of chervil
1/2 cup cream, scalded
Chicken stock (optional)

Boil the potatoes (skins on) until just soft. Remove the skins and slice.

Sauté the chopped onions in the butter until wilted. Combine with the sliced potatoes in a soup pot. Add the tomatoes, water, and seasonings.

Simmer for an hour, then add the scalded cream.

If necessary, thin the soup with more cream or chicken stock. Correct seasonings. Serve very hot.

Serves eight.

HARLEY'S AUNT JANE'S TYPICAL MENU

Sautéed Calf's Liver

Carrot Ring with Petit Pois

Prune Whip

Lordy, no wonder she weighed seventy pounds. As far as we know, Aunt Jane never actually went into her kitchen. She "planned meals," and they were delicious—if somewhat scanty. Aunt Jane was intent on keeping her girlish figure. And Gayden's children always wanted to go to lunch there!

CHAPTER III

The Religion of the Southern Mother:
Ancestor Worship with a Thin
Christian Veneer

ONCE UPON A TIME, a Greenville mother went to Memphis to attend a lecture on the ancient Medes and Persians. After the talk, all a-titter, she approached the lecturer. "I must tell you," she said, barely suppressing the urge to boast, "the Meads are my third cousins, on Daddy's side."

Ancestor worship is Mother's religion. It was the author Hamilton Basso who compared this to Shinto, a Japanese religion that is also heavy on the ancestors, and noted "the thin Christian veneer." A good Southern dawtah can spout the family tree by the age of five. As the standard bearer of civilization, Mother has taught her to do this. The Southerner never needs to go to ancestry.com to find out who her great-great-grandfather was. Mother has told us. Repeatedly. Our obsession with our antecedents may seem snobbish to the non-Southerner, but that would be the wrong way to look at our ancestor fetish. Up to a point.

We remember the trenchant observation of the author Florence King, whose book *Confessions of a Failed Southern Lady* describes her grandmother's heartbreaking attempts to turn Miss King into a DAR. She noted that whenever Southerners feel down, they just think about their illustrious ancestors. This peps us up. We even give them promotions: Yeoman farmers become knights, and knights, if depression persists, become royal dukes. Nothing makes a Southerner feel better than descent from a duke, unless it is direct descent from a bastard son of a king of England. Some of us belong to the Society for the Bastard Children of Kings of England. We have a dear friend who persists in referring to "the other Boleyn girl" as "Granny."

A Southerner can gauge the state of her mental health by how often she finds herself perusing her Colonial Dames papers. Even in the best of times, the charts are tempting reading. When the Dames did a book on Mississippi families, one of our dear mothers proclaimed it "the best book I've ever read." (The competition was stiff: an entire library of Harlequin romances.) We don't care if nobody outside the city limits (or even inside the city limits, for that matter) gives a hoot who we are—we know. That is enough. A Southerner is never lost in the cosmos. Who was it who said, "Lookin' at my pedigree charts is more curative than Zoloft and a double Scotch"? We feel certain it was a Southern mama.

Sometimes Southern mothers do too good a job of endowing their daughters with a sense of their elevated lineage. "When I go into the antique store on Royal Street," one Greenville belle who'd moved to New Orleans gushed, "I just tell them who I am and they are so nice to me."

"Who," our catty friend Alice Hunt demanded, "do you tell them you are?"

We know a poor Southern daughter who became hysterical after cutting herself on the arm. She wasn't sobbing because of the cut, which was little more than a scratch. No, there was another reason. "Mama, it ain't blue," the distraught four-year-old sobbed. She knew she was a blue blood because, after all, she was one of the biggest trailer park heiresses in the entire South.

As you may gather, there is sometimes an element of denial present in ancestor worship. But all in all, it is a good thing. It instills standards. It makes us hold our heads high. Closely related to ancestor worship is the Southerner's obsession with manners. After the late hostilities, good manners were all some Southerners had left. We were like the fallen class of English people who had lost their money and power and only had their upper-class accents—their aitches—to keep them going. Southerners held onto good manners for dear life, and we survived. The Southern mother today feels that the most important thing she can do is create tiny ladies and gentlemen who grow up to be like Melanie and Ashley (only with more gumption than Ashley) in *Gone with the Wind*. (In her heart of hearts she prefers Scarlett and Rhett—that is the Southern mother's secret dark side.)

Nice Southern mothers are fond of reminding their children that a lady can speak to anybody. A lady takes pains never to hurt the feelings of her social inferiors—a very large class of people indeed if Mama has done a good enough job on Melanie. Be sweet, Mama telegraphs, if her daughter initially hesitates to gush over old Mr. So-and-So who looks like he got the day off collecting rent under the bridge. If an old lady is sufficiently hideous, Mama will invite her for a Sunday ride and make us go along so all our friends see us. We must be sweet if we know what is good for us. Mother, who is genuinely fond of old Mrs. Ugly, knows this will make us better people—and she is right. "Some day," she says, "you will thank me." And, some day, we do.

As with ancestor worship, denial is a very important component of Southern manners. We learned about denial because of the late hostilities, too, when proper Southern ladies were going around thinking: "You don't mean to say we lost? Surely, we won. Well, in a way, we did, because now we just don't notice half the awful things that go on in the world." As we have mentioned, the proper response to anything unpleasant: "This just isn't happening." It makes us crazy. But we are nice crazy. Sometimes it is difficult not to notice unpleasant aspects of life. If, for example, there is a fly in your soup, and you're at somebody else's house, you pretend it's not floating in the rimmed bowl or bouillon cup, with the proper spoon chosen according to whether it's cream, clear, or perhaps a chunky vegetable soup. That, for the daughter of a Southern mother, is what's important: the proper soup spoon. Saying, "There's a big, ugly, dead fly in my soup, waiting to be scooped up with my oval dessert/ soup spoon," might make the hostess feel bad. Nobody wants to treat their guests to fly à la crème. And, anyway, it's not really there.

Alice Hunt once went to a Bohemian party in New York where she spotted a roach crawling out from under a hunk of herb-encrusted Brie. "I knew that I was the only person there whose mama had brought her up right," recalled Alice, who feels superior to the Yankees, among whom she has chosen to pass her days. Instead of pointing out that Mr. Real Kill survivor was competing for the *fromage,* Alice waited slyly for the inferior Yankees to spot the not-so-wee bug—and when they did, not being Southern ladies and gentlemen, some of them shrieked. Alice Hunt couldn't get over the rudeness. She was glad her mama had brought her up to be a lady. She was furthermore thankful that she'd stopped eating the Brie a half hour earlier. Good manners, as this illustrates, have a utilitarian value.

The element of denial demanded by Southern mothers can be seen in the saga of Cousin Edward de Graffenreid. The de Graffenreids are a very old family who live in the country, near Greenville. (Our friend Augusta would have killed to get one of those de's—even if Augusta de Pitts doesn't have quite the same ring.) One summer Mary Alice de Graffenreid piled all the children into the station wagon to drive cross-country and meet all the heretofore unmet de Graffenreids. When the de Graffenreids reached Mobile, Mary Alice called an elderly cousin named Katie de Graffenreid. Cousin Katie was delighted, and allowed as how her favorite restaurant was the Piccadilly, a cafeteria. Then she asked, "May I bring Edward de Graffenreid?" Mary Alice was thrilled, especially as the distinguished old gentleman wasn't on her original list of de Graffenreids. "Please do," she said enthusiastically.

When Cousin Katie and Edward de Graffenreid showed up at the Piccadilly, Mary Alice was forced to glower at the children to prevent them from commenting on the obvious: Edward de Graffenreid was a parrot. Cousin Katie, who, truth to tell (which Southerners try not to do), seemed a little dotty, appeared to regard Edward de Graffenreid as a full-fledged member of the human race. Mary Alice was determined not to hurt the old lady's feelings. It was soon apparent that Cousin Katie and Edward de Graffenreid were regulars at the Piccadilly. This could be ascertained from the pained expressions on the faces of the waitstaff and also from Cousin Katie's and Edward de Graffenreid's vocal familiarity with the menu, about which they engaged in lively—and loud (both were stone deaf)—chatter all the way down the cafeteria line. "Edward doesn't like lime Jell-O," the old lady said. "Edward de Graffenreid doesn't care for marshmallows, either," she added definitively. The bird agreed, at the top of its bird lungs. "Edward de Graffenreid doesn't like marshmallows. . . . Edward de Graffenreid doesn't like lime Jell-O," the parrot shrieked. Rude people, presumably children of Yankee mothers, stared. Johnny de Graffenreid, eight, was trying to hide himself behind the coatrack, when Mary Alice fixed him with one of her celebrated if-looks-could-kill killer looks. Without a Southern mother, Johnny might have let on that Cousin Edward was a parrot and that Cousin Katie was a few short of a full deck, spoiling the old lady's understandably rare outings, instead of patiently feeding the greedy bird bits of fried okra.

"See no faux pas" might be the Southern mother's version of "see no evil." Or rather pretend you see no faux pas. Our mothers have taught us never to say: "*That* fork, Mrs. Jones." That might hurt Mrs. Jones's feelings. Nice people wait patiently until the fork sinner has gone home, and *then* we indulge ourselves. We ask: "Where was Mrs. Jones raised, in a barn?" This is perfectly acceptable and, indeed, is tactful in the extreme. In addition to providing a modicum of entertainment for denizens of a part of the world that doesn't get first-run movies, Southern mothers have long appreciated the educational value of talking bad about people behind their backs. "When setting the table," a Memphis mother explained, "you place the knives with the sharp edge pointing inward. If you do it incorrectly, people will talk bad about you." Having had all this drummed into them at an early age, DSMs always unwrap their plastic utensils at Wendy's; they then set their places properly. They also put diapers—little napkins wrapped around the bottom—on their cheeseburgers.

Lavinia Highsmith is widely praised as having instilled the rules in her children. "You have to be nice, no matter what," she always told them. She generally said this about a hundred times when the annoying George Filson, a little boy known as being somewhat less than perfect, was coming to play. One day, when George was visiting, the Highsmith girls left him alone on the side porch with their aquarium for too long. When the girls finally remembered to check on George—who had been unusually quiet for a suspiciously long period of time—they were horrified to discover that he had removed all the fish from the tank and filleted them. First he lied and said somebody else had done it. Then he admitted that he had done it but with good reason: "We don't have any appetizers," he pointed out. The stricken girls wanted to cry. But that might not be nice. George's feelings might be hurt, and he would go through life as a fish murderer. Instead of retaliating, Precious Highsmith, seven, went to the kitchen to whip up vinaigrette. If the girls were going to have to eat Mr. and Mrs. Finny, garlic-infused olive oil might make them go down more easily. Fortunately, Miss Lavinia drove up with Happy Meals just in the nick of time. Happy Meals, she explained, don't require appetizers. She was tempted to raise her voice and speak harshly to George, but that would be unrefined. In child-rearing, Southern mothers much prefer mild forms of sadism (such as the guilt-inducing you-have-disappointed-me chat) to being unrefined.

When Lavinia—not usually an early riser, preferring to dally in bed until around lunchtime—decided one morning to arise early and prepare breakfast for the children, refinement was the keynote. She would make it a teaching moment. The glasses—juice glasses and crystal water goblets—sparkled in the morning light. A damask tablecloth set off the polished silver. She prepared shad roe, a dish from olde Virginny. The children were frantic not to miss the school bus, and they had never seen shad roe, which didn't look too appealing in the dawn's early light. This time the children did break down and sob. When the school bus honked, and the four angry children fled, Lavinia herself dissolved in tears, tears of self-pity: What kind of children didn't like shad roe? "Tacky children" was the only answer that came to mind. Should she get out the Colonial Dame charts and search for some redneck ancestor who made them this way? Didn't they *know*?

This highlights the strange schizophrenia of the Southern mother when it comes to instilling manners. While she spends every waking moment torturing her children about their manners, she also somehow expects her children to have been born knowing the finer points of etiquette. She is shocked when they don't.

We remember when one of our friends had an epiphany the night before the Delta Debutante ball—for many Delta mothers a moment only a few notches below Precious Baby's wedding: "I don't know how to curtsey," she suddenly realized. Genuinely upset, she rushed to inform her mother for comfort and solace. But that is not what she received. "Any fool can curtsey," Mo-thuh said, glowering. "Well, yes," Alice Hunt, who can never resist saying something mean, said, "I know the other girls can curtsey, but what about me?"

Not all Southern mothers think their daughters are going to grow up to be Mrs. Astor, but at an early age they do start the training—just in case. Piano, ballet, and art lessons run the gamut. "You were taught never to chew gum, smoke standing up, or go out in rollers," said a DSM. "And you never went to church without a hat, or at least a chapel cap." Some mothers laid down the law that there was only one place gum could be chewed: under the bed. (The Rollers Rule was sometimes broken when girls used them as fake-a-dates—you drove all over town in rollers, giving the impression you had a hot date that night. Mother would appreciate the craftiness, if not the rollers.) Piercing your ears and dyeing your hair were also forbidden, though there were rebels. We all remember when Shirley from Leland dyed her hair pink for a dance . . . to match her sequined dress. We think her family had beauty parlor connections.

The Victorians, it is said, invented fish knives and forks just to make trouble for those they regarded as arrivistes. We feel that God actually invented such an array of pieces of silver to give the Southern mother a sense of mission. We realize that just as Precious may not become Mrs. Astor, she probably won't be using finger bowls on a daily basis either. But some Southern mothers, when doing mother-daughter silver polishing (a highly regarded form of mother-daughter bonding), instruct their daughters in the more esoteric pieces of silver and such matters as the finger bowl. "What would you do if the Queen of England were coming to dinner?" is a question Delta mamas often ask. It is a rhetorical question, this being unlikely, unless the royal family takes up catfish farming. But you need to know, don't you?

One little girl in Leland didn't realize this was a rhetorical device. "I have to go home for lunch," she explained to her third-grade teacher, "because the Queen of England is coming." This threw all Leland into a frenzy of anticipation. But the point is that if you do get invited to the palace, as the famous London hostess Marguerite Littman, who was born right down the road in Arkansas, frequently is, you would not drink from the finger bowls.

If a daughter doesn't sit up straight, hold up her end in the conversation, and navigate the silver correctly, the mother has vowed, "I'll stab you under the table with a fork." A very naughty Southern daughter referred to mothers who say this as "mother-forkers"; if her own mother had caught on—or admitted she'd caught on—this daughter would have been punished severely, no doubt by the Southern mother's sadistic practice of behaving as if she has been stabbed in the heart with a fork whenever she is disappointed by her descendants. Kicking an offender under the table, pinching elbows, or sticking thumbs in the back while innocently passing the table are also standard operating procedures for the Southern mother. One Southern son claims he was scarred for life by Mother's constantly licking her handkerchief and wiping his face in the car before they went out in public. But he was such a nice little boy that old ladies always wanted to kiss him, and Mother had to furtively wipe away their lipstick.

Table manners, incidentally, aren't limited to the above. Southern daughters never sit like a bump on a log—they make conversation. Says a Southern mother, "I tell my children that nobody invites them to a party because they think they need a meal. They invite them to be interesting and contribute to the evening." Southern daughters may not sing for their supper—and then again, they might—but they will do almost anything to be amusing, even if it means spilling the secrets of everybody they know. Gossip is a life skill all good Southern mothers impart to their daughters. In this, our mothers taught by example. Think of it as the fishin' factor. Southern mothers are always in fishin' mode (not the kind with a rod and reel). They will (innocently, according to them) repeat anything. Gossip is an Olympic sport down here. We have watched our mothers trade up and down for juicy tidbits: "I saw Porter Jones driving down Washington Avenue," Mother might say, baiting her hook, "with a blond lady who didn't look a bit like Meri-Dell Jones. Now, who do you think it might have been?" If Mother is in hot pursuit of your deepest, darkest secret, she hints that repression will cause you to develop neurotic tics later; you are afraid to counter that, if you tell her, she will develop a neurotic tic *now*.

As you can see, the Southern mother is a highly competitive creature. She may have honed her skills in baton twirling or stealing other girls' beaux. We don't know which. It is also unclear if she is competitive *for* her children—or *through* her children. We only know that her competitive juices flow stronger than the Mississippi River. Above all, she wants her daughter to be popular. Sally Tennyson's mother shot Sally right to the top in the first grade. Sally had the biggest, fullest skirts *and* the most perfect curls. It was such an issue at Carrie Stern Elementary

School that one mother called Big Sally to learn her secret. She said she soaked Sally's petticoats in clear gelatin! They stayed puffed *all* day and, of course, Sally was the most popular girl in the reading circle. We start early in the South. It should not come as a shock that Delta mothers encourage Mary Kay parties. The Mary Kay rep, a popular member of our community, drives up in her pink Cadillac and spreads a vast selection of products—as she calls them—on the dining room table. Before long, the girls have applied so much eyeliner that they look like raccoons. Is Mother dismayed? Not a bit. She knows that Miss Priss is acquiring essential life skills that aren't formally taught in school, unless you are in beautician school. We feel certain that Tammy Faye Bakker is smiling down from heaven.

Speaking of Tammy Faye, Southern mothers are obsessed with church and Sunday school. Sundays are the worst day of the week for children of Southern mothers. Mother might not make it herself—she may need her beauty rest. One Southern mother we know attended church so infrequently that when she did, her siblings called around town and asked, "Did you hear about the explosion at the 'piscopal church? Myrtle went to church this Sunday and it fell down." But Myrtle's daughters had perfect attendance. St. James is full of members now of a certain age who have enough in the way of pins, wreaths, and dangling gilt bars—each denoting a year of perfect attendance— to impersonate a Latin American dictator. For some reason, it is very important to Mother that her children arrive in their pew on time.

Mrs. Robert Shaw, who considered leaving her estate to the Billy Graham Crusade, was a particularly devout mother, but not so much so that she wanted to get up at daybreak—defined as any hour before lunch—and go to church. She sent her children with the handyman. It didn't take Roberta Shaw long to figure out that nobody would be the wiser if she got Buster to drop her at the marina instead of the church, and so she grew up to be a pagan rather than a Presbyterian. Thank heavens her mother never knew. During the teenage and college years, church attendance may become more problematical. But Mother is unwavering. Mother's rubric, to use a term from the *Book of Common Prayer,* is that you have to go to church, no matter how hungover you are. If you can stay up all night, Mother says, you sure as hell can get to church.

Almost as important as attendance, in Mother's eyes, if perhaps not in God's, is the proper Sunday attire. We are not a society in which flip-flops are deemed divine on Sunday. Little girls must have bows in their hair and yokes with elaborate smocking; if a great aunt went blind doing the smocking, it is only that much more meaningful. Smocked yokes can be handed down to little sisters.

Like mothers elsewhere, the Southern mother sometimes has a hard time realizing that little Precious is getting older. Unlike most mothers elsewhere, she is quite likely to dress Precious herself every morning until Precious starts applying to colleges. She sometimes makes Precious wear children's clothes when Precious wants a strapless. Dinwiddie Highsmith (this is our idea of a nice girl's name) was thirteen when she was chosen to be a page at the Holly Ball. The ball is in Little Rock and Dinwiddie lives in the country. Determined that Dinwiddie would look as elegant as any of the city girls, Lavinia bought her a beautiful dress with a sash with roses embroidered on it and insisted that Dinwiddie put her feet—which were attached to legs as yet unacquainted with Lady Schick—in short white cotton socks and Mary Janes. The ensemble was completed by pipe cleaners bent into a Santa Claus motif in Dinwiddie's hair. There is debate as to whether the pipe cleaners featured blinking lights. Out Dinwiddie went, hairy legs and all, excited to be welcomed into the society of city girls. It was not to be. Dinwiddie's heart sank when she saw the other girls. They tottered on heels, did not have hirsute legs, and wore sophisticated frocks, protected against the winter weather by their mothers' minks. No pipe cleaners, it should be noted, crowned their heads. Dinwiddie made an indelible impression that night—just not the right one.

When Baby Doll, Lavinia's younger daughter, also at the age of thirteen, was invited to be a page at the Delta Debutante Club a few years later, Lavinia vowed not to repeat her mistake. She whisked Baby Doll to Memphis to buy high heels and a black dress, suggestively low cut in the back, with rhinestone buttons. Instead of pipe cleaners, Baby Doll sported in her elaborately coiffed hair a plume of egret feathers. No, Lavinia's daughters would never again be country come to town. As God was her witness. Unfortunately, Greenville *is* the country, or at least more the country than Little Rock. As she walked into the ballroom of the Greenville Country Club, Baby Doll was confronted by a horrible sight—a bevy of pages in their cotton socks and pipe cleaner tiaras, with their unshaven legs. "Yerger Wright looked at me like I was hen droppings," Baby Doll recalls bitterly.

The Delta Debutante Club is one of the many networking groups beloved of Delta mothers. Some mothers think of it as social and others regard it as Behavioral Science 101—or the place where their girls get a big lesson in behaving properly for all occasions. It was started by the late Mrs. Judge Rabun Jones, one of the Delta's great ladies and most venerable hostesses (even if she did once leave her false teeth in boiling water, giving a strange aroma to her party for a young bride). It is run by a committee of respected ladies, who meet to discuss the coming year's debutantes over sherry and, if they have not had too much sherry, remember to send the invitations. Mrs. Hazleton, a pillar of the organization, was famous for being vague. She once asked Laura Finney's little sister, "Is that Laura Finney a nice young lady?"

"Whenever I have to face a business meeting I don't want to go to," said one former debutante who now lives in the North, "I just say to myself, 'Get out there and curtsey, no matter how scared you are.' It works every time." Like many debs of that era—the sixties—she had pretended that she was just doing it for Mama. It's true, Mama would have committed suicide if she hadn't. But all Delta girls harbor a secret dream of dancing drunk on tables in honky-tonks during their debutante year. Mother harbors a dream that they won't. Mama sees it as an opportunity for her daughter to practice doing the most important thing in life—replying in kind to invitations. If an invitation is formal, we reply formally. We know one Delta grandmother whose granddaughter lived on the West Coast. When it came time for the granddaughter to marry, "Don't put reply cards in any invitations you send to Greenville," she ordered her daughter. "We still know how to do the right thing here."

Other networking opportunities are Dirt Daubers, the garden club for girls who are not quite old enough to go to Mary Kay parties; Sub Deb; and Junior Cotillion. Delta mothers don't care if their daughters hate every minute of it, they want them to join. At the very least, they learn how to cope with other vicious teenage girls. Mother, alas, often cares more than her daughter. When one daughter was not invited to Junior Cotillion, she was quite relieved. Such a bore! Mother was not relieved. Mother got on the phone and called everybody with a similar last name in the entire Delta to see if an invitation had mistakenly been delivered to them. Each call was the same: "Hello, this is Mary Sue Ames. I was Mary Sue Hill. My daddy was . . . I wonder if by chance a letter to my daughter has been sent to you by mistake. Um huh. Um huh. I see. Well, thank you so much. . . ." "Hello, this is Mary Sue Ames. I was . . ." And so it went, until she ran out of phone books.

Southern mothers teach their children to network early. After play group, a good opportunity to meet "nice" children, comes day school, starting at two. Parents fill out forms (sometimes pre-birth) for the correct day school. But isn't this just like in New York? No, New Yorkers are trying to get their children into Ivy League schools. We are not; educational benefits are low on the totem pole for a Southern mother. As one mother made the mistake of saying (when I asked why she wanted her child to go to St. James), "The right people are in the carpool lane." We know one mother who enrolled her child in CAR (the kiddie version of DAR) at the age of two months. Most mothers wait until the child is nine or ten.

There is one area in which Southern mothers often fail to educate their young properly: money matters. Southern mothers often have skewed financial wisdom that they pass on to their young. It is the decimal point that gives the Southern mother so much difficulty. When Dora Parker's uncle—who was a big shot at the bank—called Dora, mother of three, to tell her she was overdrawn, she felt awful. "Oh, Uncle Buddy," she said. "I'm embarrassed to death. I'll write a check this minute to cover it." Here, in a nutshell, we see the Southern mother's brand of financial wisdom. "How could I be overdrawn?" another Delta mother in a similar situation wondered. "I still have three checks." The Southern mother may not always spend wisely, but when something is really important to her, she astounds you. When one Southern mother we know got her divorce, she went to the bank that day and started a savings account for

Sistuh's debut. It is significant that she didn't think to start a college fund.

As we have noted, we all become our mothers. When it comes to manners, we do this at an early stage in life. Elizabeth Shackelford at an early age attained fame (and horrified her mother) by perfecting the art of burping her ABCs. "All children are inherently tacky," said a Delta mother. Proving this wisdom, Elizabeth let go with one of her signature burps at the country club. Grandfather Duke Shackelford, glasses sliding down his nose, looked at her in silent disapproval. It was tense until little Mary Grace, six, piped up: "Elizabeth Shackelford," she said in a tiny voice, "here we are in the politest place in town, and you burp." "Southern motherhood," said Lucy Shackelford, Elizabeth's mother, "begins at the age of six."

But do we, as Mother predicted, grow up and thank her? We do. In a world where people are asked by their employers to sign up for courses with names like Everyday Etiquette for the Office, we are glad Mama has already taught us what to do. We are also glad that we learned early on to be nice to old ladies—and old men—just because they are old. Although Mama often dwelled on the finer points of good manners, she also taught us that good manners are nothing more than being considerate of others. It is certainly more pleasant to dine with somebody who doesn't talk with her mouth open and makes conversation. Simple, thoughtful manners have endured, and that is in no small part because of our mothers. So, yes, we are grateful that we had Southern mothers.

THE SOUTHERN MOTHER'S (CHICKEN!) BREAST FETISH

OUR MOTHERS would go around the world to avoid saying the word "breast"—except when it referred to a chicken's breast. Southern mothers love chicken breasts. Forget the rest of the poor bird. Southern mothers teach their daughters that it's white meat only! In the old days, when Father sat at the head of the table and served plates, he'd sooner have given his Precious Baby arsenic than something other than a breast. The drumsticks were reserved for children. Chicken salad and all the finer chicken dishes require breasts in the Deep South, at least for the ladies. All these recipes are delicious—and none of them is going to win a prize from the Pritikin Center.

Buttermilk Fried Chicken

*T*here's a dark side to the white meat fetish: Southern ladies realize that, no matter how much of the meat they eat, the fried, crunchy skin is what they really like. Also, anything cooked with the bone in it always tastes better. You can pretty much figure that anything that tastes good is bad for you.

Somewhere along the way it became fashionable to cover up our food. You could not find your chicken breast. Then some years later the poor thing got stripped of everything other than the hormones to plump it up. All the good tasty stuff was replaced by killer chemicals. I'd rather have the skin. With this recipe, you'll get good crunchy skin. Most Southern cooks prefer a well-seasoned skillet to an electric fryer.

．　　　．　　　．

Ingredients
6 chicken breasts
Buttermilk
2 eggs
2 cups whole milk
2 cups flour

Salt to taste
Pinch of garlic powder
Black pepper to taste
¼ teaspoon baking powder
Fat for frying (Crisco, vegetable oil, or a combination)

Soak the breasts overnight in buttermilk. Beat the eggs and blend the beaten eggs with the whole milk, then dip the chicken in the mixture. Combine the flour, salt, garlic powder, pepper (a generous amount), and baking powder in a brown grocery bag or, if you want to be au courant, ziplock bag, and shake to mix. Shake the chicken, one piece at a time, in the bag until well coated. (At this point, some cooks like to remove the chicken pieces, dip them in the eggs, and repeat the egg-wash-and-flour procedure.)

Using a preseasoned black-iron skillet, heat enough of the fat to almost cover the chicken. When you drop the chicken in, the fat should sizzle. The art of frying involves the grease, which must not burn the chicken but cooks it at an even, medium-hot level. Do not crowd the chicken when frying. Turn only once, when golden brown on one side. Remove from the skillet and drain on a brown grocery bag that has been covered with a layer of paper towels, approximately 20 minutes.

Serves six.

Country Captain

Country Captain is a recipe with English roots. It is believed to have been named for a captain in the India service. That must be why we Delta Anglophiles love it, though it may be too informal to serve when Queen Elizabeth comes to dinner. This recipe is adapted from one that belonged to the late Mrs. Roger Bostick and first appeared in *Gourmet of the Delta*.

．　　　・　　　・

Ingredients

4 to 6 chicken breasts, depending on the size of the bosom
Fat (Crisco or vegetable oil)
1/2 cup flour
4 cups water
1/2 cup mushrooms
2 1/2 cups tomatoes
1/2 cup minced onion
1/4 teaspoon thyme
1 1/2 teaspoons salt
1 cup green peas
3/4 cup celery, chopped
1/2 clove garlic

1 teaspoon curry powder
Cooked rice
Almonds and/or cooked currants

Brown the breasts in fat. Leaving about ½ cup fat in the skillet, remove the breasts. Add the flour to the fat, stirring. Pour in the water gradually, making gravy. Add the mushrooms, tomatoes, onion, thyme, salt, peas, celery, garlic, and curry powder. Return the chicken to the mixture. Cover and cook 30 to 40 minutes. It should be served over rice with the almonds and/or currants on top.

Serves four to five.

King Ranch Chicken

$\mathcal{M}$any of our mothers did not cook with tortilla chips. In this recipe, the elegance of tortilla chips is enhanced with Cheez Whiz and cream of mushroom soup. Try to think of this as a downscale version of Country Captain—way downscale. Just about the only nice thing to be said about King Ranch Chicken is that it's one of the best things you'll ever eat.

.   .   .

Ingredients
6 cooked chicken breasts
1 can cream of chicken soup
1 can cream of mushroom soup
1 onion, chopped
1 can (10 ounces) tomatoes with green chillies
1 jar (8 ounces) Cheez Whiz
Dash of Tabasco
Dash of Lea & Perrins Worcestershire Sauce
Salt and pepper
Tortilla chips, crushed
8 ounces Cheddar
4 ounces mozzarella

Dice the cooked chicken breasts. Preheat oven to 350°. In a saucepan over medium heat, mix the soups, onion, tomatoes, Cheez Whiz, Tabasco, and Worcestershire Sauce until blended. Add salt and pepper to taste. Line the bottom of a casserole dish with the crushed tortilla chips. Place the chicken on top and pour over some of the mixture. Add a layer of half the Cheddar. Repeat the process, topping with Cheddar and mozzarella.

Serves six.

Proustian Chicken

*O*ne of the popular chicken dishes Charlotte remembers fondly from childhood featured mushrooms and sherry. The recipe has been lost to posterity, but after some tinkering, we came up with this, which is quite close—and brings back memories.

*   *   *

Ingredients
6 chicken breasts
Salt, pepper, and flour
2/3 stick butter
2 cloves garlic
1 can (4 ounces) mushrooms, sliced and drained
1 cup sherry
Paprika (for color)

Salt, pepper, and flour the breasts lightly. Mix the butter and garlic in a frying pan. Brown the chicken in this, but not for too long. Remove the chicken from the pan. Add the mushrooms to the pan. Add the sherry and stir well. Return the chicken breasts to the pan and baste them. Cook in a 325° oven for an hour. Sprinkle on the paprika to add some color before serving.

Serves six.

Chicken Breast Piccata

*G*etting good veal in parts of the South is almost impossible. Improvisation was in order. So we invented Chicken Piccata. The addition of capers or curry was an exotic touch that gave our mothers the idea that they were thereby more worldly, slightly international. Maybe this dish should be called I Can't Believe It's Not Veal Piccata!

* * *

Ingredients
1¹/₂ to 2 pounds boneless chicken breasts
¹/₂ cup all-purpose flour
Salt and freshly ground pepper to taste
¹/₄ cup butter
1 tablespoon olive oil
Juice of 1 lemon
2 tablespoons capers
3 tablespoons chopped parsley
2 cloves garlic

Put the chicken between pieces of waxed paper and pound thin. Lightly flour the chicken, season with salt and pepper, and then lightly sauté in ⅛ cup butter and olive oil. Cook on each side. Place on a warm platter. Add remaining butter and the lemon juice to the skillet. Add the (drained) capers, parsley, and garlic. Be sure to scrape the delicious tidbits of chicken off the bottom. Nap the chicken with this sauce.

Serves six.

Stained Glass Manor Curried Chicken Breasts

A real Southern cook cooks by tasting...a little of this, a dash of that. We don't measure as much as good cooks elsewhere. This recipe should probably be called Drive Yankee Cooks Crazy Curried Chicken Breasts! Shirley Smollen of the Stained Glass Manor, a B and B in Vicksburg, Mississippi, says that the only ingredient for which she can give a specific measure is the butter—a whole stick. The B and B is in the residence of Fannie Vicks Johnson, whose family gave Vicksburg its name. The late Mrs. Johnson, who is kin to Shirley, often visits her old house. We hope she still enjoys the big, quiet front porch.

. . .

Ingredients
1 big apple (or two little apples), cubed
1 big onion, diced
Several tablespoons curry powder
1 stick butter
Rice
3 chicken breasts, cubed

Mix all but the chicken and the rice together and sauté in the butter. While sautéing, stir-fry the cubed chicken until it is completely done. No color, as nothing is worse than insufficiently cooked chicken. Then combine the chicken and mixture in one big pan and cook for a few minutes over a low heat. Serve over rice. Shirley uses only Ellis Stansel Rice from Gueydan, Louisiana, which can be ordered in small bags from the producer. It smells a bit like popcorn when cooked. Shirley prefers ordinary grocery store curry to more exotic Indian kinds.

Serves six.

Mrs. Humphreys McGee's Chicken Spaghetti

*C*ould it be that this recipe's call for *tiny* English peas is a subtle attempt to upgrade chicken spaghetti from its déclassé status? Chicken spaghetti is one of those dishes that we love and eat readily—but we might not tell everybody. The late Mrs. Humphreys McGee, whose husband was so beloved at Sewanee that the athletic field bears his name, dared to share her recipe!

. . .

Ingredients
1 large hen, stewed until very tender
4 medium onions, chopped
3 large bell peppers, chopped
3 cups chopped celery
3 cloves garlic, minced
Bacon drippings
1 can tomatoes
1 can Rotel tomatoes
1 can tomato soup
1 can tiny English peas
2 cans sliced mushrooms
1 teaspoon salt

1 teaspoon black pepper
3/4 teaspoon cayenne pepper
2 tablespoons Lea & Perrins Worcestershire Sauce
  (optional replacement for salt and peppers)
28 ounces capellini
Grated sharp Cheddar cheese
Parmesan cheese

Using scissors, cut the hen into small pieces. Simmer the on-ions, peppers, celery, and garlic in the bacon grease until tender. Add the tomatoes, soup, peas, mushrooms, and chicken and cook slowly until done. Season with the salt and the black and red pepper (or Worcestershire Sauce). Cook the capellini in salted boiling water. It should be done but firm. Place the capel-lini in a colander and run hot water over it. Put a somewhat thick layer of capellini into a large mixing bowl and cover with the sauce, adding a generous layer of grated Cheddar cheese. Repeat this process until everything is used. Allow it to set a few minutes, and then mix gently, stirring from the bottom, with a wooden fork or spoon. This should be served very hot, with a sprinkling of parmesan cheese on each serving.

Serves around twelve.

Chicken Marbella

*Y*ou say Mar-BEY-ya—we say Mar-bella. (Come to think of it, don't we know somebody named Marbella?) What's undeniable is that this dish is marbelous! It is aromatic and tasty.

. . .

Ingredients

1/2 cup olive oil
1/2 cup red wine vinegar
1/2 cup pitted green olives
1/2 cup capers with juice
1 cup pitted prunes
5 bay leaves
1 whole head of garlic, peeled and chopped
1/4 cup dried oregano
5 chicken breasts, boneless and skinless
Salt
Freshly ground pepper
1/4 cup brown sugar
1 cup dry white wine
Chopped parsley

Combine the olive oil, vinegar, olives, capers and a small amount of their juice, prunes, bay leaves, garlic, and oregano. Stir gently to slightly mix.

Place the chicken in a bowl and lightly salt and pepper. Pour the above mixture over the chicken, being sure that all the chicken is coated. Cover and refrigerate overnight (at least).

To cook:

Heat the oven to 350°. Place the chicken in a shallow baking dish and cover with the marinade. Lightly sprinkle with the brown sugar. Add the white wine. Baste frequently using the pan juices. Cook 1 hour or until the chicken is done.

Remove the chicken to a serving platter and spoon the marinade with pan juices over the top. Garnish with chopped parsley.

Serves five.

Exotic Chicken Salad

*T*his recipe comes from our friend Dee Whitley, who lives in California, but it is similar to salads our mothers served. It would be perfect for a summer luncheon. A variation from Dee's recipe, since Southerners think that artichoke hearts are the height of elegance, is to substitute canned artichoke hearts for the pineapple. White Thompson grapes go nicely in this recipe.

·   ·   ·

Ingredients
1 large can water chestnuts
2 quarts coarsely cut chicken breast
2 cups sliced celery
2 to 3 cups slivered almonds
2 pounds seedless grapes
1 large pineapple, cut into tidbits
3 cups mayonnaise
1/2 to 1 tablespoon curry powder
2 tablespoons soy sauce

Slice the water chestnuts and mix with the chicken. Add the celery and 2/3 of the almonds. Add the grapes and pineapple. If they are large grapes, slice them in half. Mix the mayonnaise, curry powder, and soy sauce and combine with the chicken mixture. Chill for several hours. Scoop onto lettuce and sprinkle with the remaining almonds.

Serves approximately eight.

TEN THINGS EVERY SOUTHERN MOTHER (SELFLESSLY) ASPIRES TO FOR HER PRECIOUS BABY

1. Christianity: Episcopalian instead of Sun Myung Moon
2. Chi Omega
3. Colonial Dames
4. Garden Club of America
5. Thin body/clear skin/perfect teeth
6. Two-story brick house
7. Perfect grandchildren
8. Junior League
9. Phi Beta Kappa (if studying doesn't get in the way of her social life!)
10. Malleable son-in-law

CHAPTER IV

❧

Mother's Two Command Modes

WHEN MARBELLA PICKETT went to spend the night at the residence of her father and meet his new wife, her mother could not contain her curiosity. Marbella's mother not only hoped that Mr. Pickett had married down, but that the second Mrs. Pickett's taste was so tacky that it made the Sears Roebuck catalog look like a tourist guidebook for Versailles (regrettably pronounced Ver-sails by some in our region). And as Marbella's mother thought about it, she realized that there was a way to satisfy her yearning for inside information: Arm Marbella with a Kodak. Though understandably reluctant, Marbella felt she had no choice but to go along with Mother's plan, and agreed to photograph her father's new house after Mr. Pickett and the "dance hall woman," as Marbella's family called the new wife (who, in reality, had never set foot in such an establishment), had gone to bed. It was perhaps not an entirely wise thing to do, but poor Mama needed a pick-me-up.

Marbella felt like a criminal sneaking around her own father's house at 3 A.M. She prayed she wouldn't be hit in the head when she went outside in pitch black dark to get a good frontal shot of the exterior. Wanting to make Mama happy, Marbella moved an ensemble of kitsch close together—it was a masterful shot featuring what Marbella judged to be a prime example of JC Penney Duncan Phyfe, set off with artificial flowers. She knew *that* would lift Mama's spirits. When Marbella returned home, she felt as if she had turned into a photographer for *Veranda,* if *Veranda* went in for cellophane-wrapped sofas. But then Mama suddenly turned cowardly and refused to take the pictures to Turner's Pharmacy to be developed. It seems that while Marbella was creeping around her father's house, Mama had been having second thoughts: What if Miss Billie, who worked at the pharmacy, saw the pictures and put two and two together? Marbella's nighttime labors might have gone for nought, but at least she could take pride in having tried to raise Mama's low spirits.

A Southern daughter always finds that she has ended up doing . . . exactly what Mama wanted her to do in the first place. Some mothers, for instance, are determined that their daughters will follow them into the Colonial Dames, even if their daughters run away to New York to escape this fate. Mama plays along. "Oh, Dabney," she will say, pretending to be sincere, "I hope you get the cutest, nicest job in New York City." She is really pulling for the nicest, cutest, most malleable stockbroker, who will bring Dabney back to Rolling Fork and build a big house next door to Mama.

While pretending an interest in Dabney's job—which, truth to tell, Mama regards primarily as conversation fodder for her bridge club, where she will inevitably describe being the receptionist in an art gallery as "arduous"—she actually focuses on more important matters: forcing Dabney to join the Dames against her will. Although the Daughters are nice, too, many mothers aim for the Dames because you have to *be invited* to join. Mother would never say this keeps the riffraff out. She doesn't have to. Dabney begs to wait until she is fifty to join, but her pleas fall, as she knew they would, on deaf ears. "You need to write a letter to Mrs. Eustace Worthington," Mother dictates, seemingly not hearing a word poor Dabney is saying, "and then send it to me to me to read before you mail it."

Why does Mother need to read the letter? After all, Mother herself has dictated it, using all the space on Dabney's voice mail: "Dear Mrs. Worthington, comma . . . new paragraph, indent, capital . . . I am writing to accept your kind . . ." She has also FedExed the correct stationery and pen, as if she thinks being out in the grubby world, among non DSMs, may cause Dabney to do something outlandish and forget the rule about Hallmark cards. (The rule can be summed up in one word: nevuh! If you receive a Hallmark sympathy card from somebody, you know she isn't a DSM.)

But back to Dabney and the Dames. Despite minutely obeying Mother's instructions, Dabney fails. It's the handwriting. A good

Southern lady's handwriting must have the look of having been written by someone who has never been in haste to communicate a thought—it must be elegant and ornamental. Under the pressures of having a job, Dabney's is taking on a utilitarian look. Mother decides it would be better if Dabney sent some blank pages, with her signature, and let Sistuh, whose penmanship is as-yet-unsullied by toil, write the actual letter.

Although a Southern mother's tones on the voice mail are dulcet, she is not to be trifled with. An iron determination lurks behind Mother's façade, even if she is one of those mothers who talks so sweet she can give you diabetes. The reason Southern mothers get away with tyranny is that they hide the iron fist in kid gloves. Silly Mama—she says the cutest things. Saying the cutest things is one of her command modes. The other is issuing orders. Either way, you can't win. When issuing orders, Mother strives for the chilling over the loud. Mother doesn't like to raise her voice. That is what fishwives do. The fishwife, by the way, looms large in Delta mythology, though very few of our mothers in the Delta, which is landlocked, have actually met many fishwives.

We did not need a feminist movement down here, because Southern women have always been in charge. They just don't let on until you're all grown up and realize that you've been downtrodden all your life. "Every mother in the county knows she runs the show," says Gayden's nephew Dickson Miller. It is, however, important that *we* don't know until it's too late to revolt. Mother has three sources of power: strength of character;

a wily knowledge of the science of psychology, sometimes known as the art of manipulation; and control of the silver and china that will go to approved members of the next generation.

You would not think, if you met the diminutive Lollie Ray—barely five feet tall, one of our favorite Delta mothers, past ninety and still beautifully turned out—that she could scare the legs off a bullfrog. But you would be wrong. When Mrs. Ray, who now lives in Dallas, recently visited her family cemetery in Helena (pronounced: Hell-na), Arkansas, and it had gone to weeds, she must have appeared bigger than a float in the Macy's parade to the quaking cemetery personnel. "I said perpetual care . . . and I meant perpetual care," she stated, without raising her voice but being chillingly scary. She stretched to attain her full five feet of grandeur. When the family went to bid farewell to the ancestors before breakfast the next day, the plot looked like Frederick Law Olmsted had just weeded it—everything was perfect. Just as Mrs. Ray had known it would be. We stand in awe. How does she do it? We also have no idea. But we know that one day, after being understudy to a pro, we will intuitively know how to do it ourselves.

"Your mother is a very determined woman," opined a shrink who had just met Olivia Morgan at a party in California. Olivia Morgan's two daughters were stunned. Was this man some kind of a quack? They had always been told that their mother was meekness personified. But who had told them this? Well, now that you mention it, it was Mama herself. The girls pondered further: Who, come to think of it, had made every major decision of their lives—from important matters such as silver patterns down to relatively minor matters such as where to go to college? Olivia Morgan. Olivia Morgan might be said to be a mistress of the indirect approach. Every time one of Olivia Morgan's husbands got a wild notion and took it into his plumb silly head that he wanted to move out of her beloved Papa's house, where Olivia Morgan dearly loved being lady of the house, Olivia Morgan said it was out of the question. She would patiently explain that she'd love to, but she had made a deathbed promise to her own dear mama to stay with Papa forever. How can you argue with that? (Actually, unpleasant Aunt Bitsy did argue, asking from time to time, "How can you make a death-bed promise to somebody who is in a coma?")

No, Mama doesn't just boss us around—that would be un-couth, not to mention being too simple. Such a straightforward course of action is not sufficiently Byzantine to appeal to the Southern mother. Here is where the trickery comes into the picture. Southern mothers often adopt a vague and/or ditzy persona. We love to tell tales about what Mama said or did. Our Yankee friends are so amused. Do Yankee mothers hear the TV weatherman talking about the windchill factor and then pour hot water on the windshield of Daddy's new Buick because they heard wind*shield* factor? Probably not, but that is what Dabney Atterbury's mother did. Isn't Mama a hoot! Olivia Morgan's daughters were also connoisseurs of her flighty sayings. Once a train passed with its capacity emblazoned on a car. "Whe-ah *is* Capa City?" Olivia Morgan asked. When Uncle Buddy bragged that he had a clean cotton crop, meaning it had few weeds, Olivia Morgan thought for a minute and then said, "Of course it's clean, Buddy. It just rained." Isn't Mama cute?

After Ann Call was diagnosed with glaucoma, she came home from the doctor expatiating on the virtues of medical marijuana. "I just don't think I can tell people my mother-in-law smokes pot," Harley Metcalfe sighed, knowing full well that his mother-in-law would do exactly what she pleased. She seemed not to have heard that marijuana was illegal. She was giddy at the mere prospect of smoking it on her toile-upholstered sofa. Is Mother really that out of it, or is it just an act? We will never know. By the time the DSM finally gets around to asking this question, she already has done everything Mama wanted her to do. Silly Mama——like a barracuda.

Long before they die Southern mothers decide who will get what pieces of the furniture. They decide and re-decide. By the time she dies, a Southern mother's will has been through more rewrites than a Hollywood script. Southern mothers make handwritten lists—again, and again and again. If you want Aunt Lottie's silver tea service, it is important to be in Mother's good graces at all times. Like many tyrants, Mother is not averse to being just. One Oxford, Mississippi, mother was frequently discovered prowling the house in her zip-up-the-front velour robe—at least one of which many of our mothers possess—at 3 A.M., with a yellow legal pad in hand—she had four daughters and three silver services. Occasionally, a Southern mother will attempt to subvert the chore of constantly adjusting The Will by tagging her belongings. We know one who reverted to The Will, however, after she stooped to pick up a fallen tag only to learn that her children were re-tagging the more desirable items. This was a not-to-be-brooked encroachment on Mother's moral authority.

The division of the spoils has an almost mystical meaning for Southern mothers. Sanctimony has been known to creep into the ritual, but this only enhances Mother's authority. We know one mother who, in the process of moving to an apartment from "the big house," summoned her four children from near and far to what became almost a church gathering. Mother placed all four in a semicircle; for an awful moment it appeared that they would be asked to hold hands and pray. But it was worse: Mother delivered a lengthy homily on the meaningless-ness of material things, a topic chosen with no hint of irony. She spoke of life as a spiritual journey; she spoke of stewardship—in fact, she spoke for a half hour. Understandably, her fidgety descendents—having already drawn lots and girded for combat—couldn't concentrate. An hour of holding hands, it must be said, did not lift their thoughts to spiritual matters—they thought only of the loot. Still, one daughter later felt that she had used the time wisely, coming up with additional reasons as to why her older sister was unworthy of the strawberry forks.

As has been noted, Mother also practices psychology without a license. She is an astute observer of her dawtah's moods. Isabelle Gordon's mother once arguably carried this too far. Isabelle came home from a party slightly tipsy. It was when her father, who had married the scarlet woman, had only a short time to live. "Buddy has died," Mrs. Gordon informed Isabelle. A few minutes later, Mrs. Gordon was forced to amend her remarks. "Well," she said, "Buddy is still with us. I just wanted to observe your reaction, and you just never know if I'll be the one to tell you."

Although the Southern mother bestirs herself to choose silver patterns, colleges, and sons-in-law, nothing looms larger than grooming and personal appearance. If a DSM "lets herself go"—the phrase is one of the most horrible in the Delta female's lexicon—Mother will regard it as a reflection on herself. "Why, what a nice picture of me at George's wedding," Olivia Morgan chirped, as she snipped off Little Olivia, who was going through a fat phase. A DSM who doesn't wear stockings to church in the equatorial heat of a Delta August risks bringing out Mama's sadistic side. "Nancy Valentine didn't have on stockings either," one DSM defiantly announced upon returning from St. James on the hottest day of the year. "Ya-yes," Mama drawled, without missing a beat, "but Nancy Valentine is thin and tanned."

A prominent Greenville dowager, Margaret Wortham Kirk, a lifelong beauty, as were her daughters, always ate her dessert first, in case she got full before finishing the main course. She and her daughters always stood immediately after eating with their backs against the dining room wall . . . to check their posture and ensure that the food didn't stop on their hips on the way to digestion. "So clearly," recalls her granddaughter,

Melinda Baskin Hudson, "this was a line of ladies who paid attention to form and honored beauty." Her grandmother carried this to the end, and no one can describe it better than Melinda: "So, Granny had a long—elegant—period of infirmity, perfectly cared for in her home by her children and entertained by her grandchildren. Her last stay in the hospital was a quiet vigil . . . her heart was not going to let her stay with us much longer. All who have sat vigil know what I mean when I say we wait for that magical and treacherous moment when, close to death, the beloved becomes suddenly and lovingly clear-eyed. . . . These are the good-byes and they soothe the soul. So when Granny opened her eyes to behold her daughter Sally, we leaned in, held our breaths. . . . 'Sally . . .' 'Yes, Mama . . .' 'Sally . . .' 'Yes, Mama, I'm here. . . .' 'Sally . . . it's a shame you didn't get your portrait done before you lost your looks.'"

Sally Baskin's Stuffed Eggs

"She was not impressed by our generation's need to do everything, and perfectly," recalls Sally Baskin's daughter, Melinda Hudson. "Being hypercompetent could only lead to trouble. Take cooking, for instance. She would say she never learned how to cook everyday food because then someone would have asked her to do it. The only dishes one needed to know how to fix were (1) something for the bereaved (stuffed eggs and fudge cake) and (2) something to make yourself useful at Christmas and Easter (oyster casserole and egg strata). Beyond that, she always said to call Amanda Cottingham at the Pantry or make a restaurant reservation.

"Now, on to stuffed eggs. It is indeed hard to imagine life without them. So important were they to one's ability to function as a part of society that when I moved to Washington, the only 'new' thing I took with me was a brand-new Lucite stuffed egg tray."

And just for the record— Sally Baskin, beautiful and charming to the last, never lost her looks.

Ingredients

4 dozen eggs

½ cup mayonnaise

1 teaspoon dry ground mustard

Salt and freshly ground pepper to taste

3 or 4 dashes of Tabasco

3 to 4 tablespoons sweet pickle relish

Paprika for garnish

"Mama's eggs were very simple," Melinda recalls. "The most important part was doing the hard boiling. Best to use old eggs (you don't hear that often), at least a week. They peel easier. Put them in a big pot, cover with cold water, toss in some salt, bring to a soft boil, take off the heat and let sit about 30 minutes (no more than 30) in the hot water. The other trick is how you cool them. After 30 minutes maximum, pour off the hot water, fill with cold water, and toss in some ice cubes. Another 20 minutes or so later, they're cool to the touch and ready to peel."

Cut the eggs in half and stuff them. (You can also cut the halves in half. You *never* have enough eggs when passed with cocktails...men love them!)

Yields forty-eight stuffed eggs.

Don't Ask, Don't Tell Potatoes

*F*rom *Country Cookin'*, self-published by Nancy Smythe Bollinger, Charlotte's cousin, who died in 2008. Nancy's cookbook radiates love of her own mother, Mayree Smythe, but this recipe comes from her sister, Lanier Smythe. It was given to Lanier by a member of a Delta family that is famous for being pencil-thin. How do they achieve it? By living on mung sprouts and beans when they aren't having Don't Ask, Don't Tell Potatoes, we assume.

. . .

Ingredients
1 pound baking potatoes
Lots of garlic
Salt and freshly ground pepper
1 cup heavy cream
2 to 4 tablespoons butter, cut into pea-size pieces

Have everything ready when you begin to peel the potatoes, so they won't have time to get discolored. Slice the potatoes very thin, in a food processor or with a mandoline. Layer them in a buttered casserole dish. Over each layer, squeeze garlic and sprinkle salt and pepper. It's best if you only do two layers, but I have done more. Pour the cream over all and dot with the butter. Bake at 300° for 1½ hours.

Serves four.

Almond Butter Crunch

*M*ae Jones, who works at the Greenville Compress, gives this as a Christmas present to the lucky directors. It's devilishly delicious.

. . .

Ingredients
1 cup sliced almonds
¹/₂ cup real butter
¹/₂ cup sugar
1 tablespoon Karo Light Corn Syrup

Butter a pizza pan and set it aside. Combine the above ingredients in a heavy saucepan.

Cook over medium high heat to boil. Boil for five or six minutes. *Stir constantly* until it turns a caramel color (be careful—this will scorch in a split second). Quickly pour into the prepared pan and spread out thinly with the back of a spoon. When hardened, wipe excess batter off with a paper towel. Break into pieces and eat just one!

Evelyn Hall's Sweet Potato Pie

S outherners love sweet potatoes—they are delicious and they've gotten us through many adversities. The *Oxford Companion to Food* notes: "The sweet potato was especially valued during the war against the British and the Civil War, for it grows quickly and its underground habit makes it less vulnerable than surface crops to deliberate destruction." No doubt, it was familiarity with the sweet potato that inspired some Southern families to bury their silver during the late hostilities.

Ingredients
1 cup mashed sweet potatoes
1 cup sugar
2 eggs
1 stick butter or margarine
1 small can PET Evaporated Milk
1 teaspoon cinnamon (or more)
1 pie crust shell

Cook the potatoes in skin. Peel and mash. Mix in other ingredients and put in unbaked pie crust shell. Bake at 350° for 50 to 60 minutes.

Serves eight.

Bourbon Soufflé

*A*s we have noted, our friend Linda Weiss studied cooking at Le Cordon Bleu in Paris, but she learned just as much from her mother, who offered this maternal dictum: "Bourbon is not just for fruitcake, my dear." This comes from a class Linda teaches at the Greenbrier, and she says it's so good you'll forget how much money you just spent at one of the South's finest hotels.

· · ·

Ingredients
4 cups milk
2 tablespoons gelatin
1 cup sugar
10 egg yolks (reserve whites separately)
1½ cups bourbon (good quality—what you would drink)
3 cups + ¼ cup whipping cream
1 cup egg whites
¼ cup sugar

Heat the milk. Mix the gelatin and sugar together and add to the hot milk, stirring as you add. Place the yolks in a bowl and add some of the hot milk mixture and mix well. Pour the egg mixture into the remaining milk mixture. Add the bourbon and cool.

When the bourbon mixture starts setting up, whip the 3 cups cream and set aside. Then whip the egg whites and sugar to make a meringue. Fold the whipped cream first, and then the meringue, into the bourbon mixture.

Take a 2-quart soufflé bowl and put a paper collar 1 inch above and 1 inch below the soufflé top. Fill the bowl with the mixture and refrigerate. After it has set for several hours, remove the collar and decorate with the remaining whipped cream. For the collar, use parchment paper or waxed paper. To hold in place, tape or string will work.

Makes one 2-quart soufflé.

CHAPTER V

A Crown in Heaven: The Southern Mother's Ultimate Passive-Aggressive Fashion Accoutrement

LTHOUGH THE Christian martyrs, whose stories we learned in Mother-mandated Sunday school, often suffered horrible fates, they have nothing on our martyrs— we mean our mothers. It is true that many of the Christian martyrs—the official ones who toiled and fought and lived and died, and were patient, brave, and true long before Mama came along—were fed to lions, run through with swords, or else disemboweled.

Well, but really, isn't that just a lot like what happened to Mrs. Hunt? She had to be rushed to the King's Daughter's Hospital for an emergency appendectomy. She contended that this very real medical crisis was triggered by embarrassment. It was brought on by the shock of noticing that Alice Hunt's Sub Deb Cotillion picture showed unmistakably that Alice had worn the wrong shoes. Snapped by Greenville's premier lens man, Flash Carson, the photograph showed Sunday pumps, not evening shoes. Mrs. Hunt wanted to die on the spot, and an emergency appendectomy was the next best thing.

Like pagan emperors, we etiquette-challenged daughters inflict pain and suffering on our Christian martyrs—mothers. An appendectomy is not quite disemboweling, you say? Well, that's hardly how Mrs. Hunt viewed it. Of course, she suffered in silence. We know because she told us. Repeatedly. Suffering and worry unending are the Southern mother's lot—and don't you forget it. Believe us, you won't. When the Greenville artsy set brought in a foreign movie, Olivia Morgan went with her daughters. She was asked the moral of a particularly gruesome Japanese film featuring numerous scenes involving hari-kari. She paused. "Honor thy mother," she offered.

As Southern daughters, we know that we have caused Mama to suffer. One time, an expatriate daughter of a Southern mother spotted a bumper sticker in Los Angeles that read: "My mother is a travel agent, specializing in guilt trips." She honked and waved enthusiastically—she just knew that the driver of a car festooned with such hard-won wisdom had to be a sister—if not an actual Chi Omega, almost certainly a fellow DSM.

We grow up with a sense of guilt because Mama suffered so much to bring us into this world and subsequently to bring us up to be ladies. "Ah gave up going out in society to take care of you when you were born," she was likely to sigh . . . as she dashed off to her bridge game, garden club, or Friends of the Library meeting (where Southern mothers make friends with each other, not the books). When we disappointed her, she spoke of the "cross I bear." Small children often heard this as the cross-eyed bear. What were our mothers doing with cross-eyed bears? Bears don't need good manners. "You will have a crown in heaven" is the Southern mother's all-time favorite compliment, implying, as it does, earthly suffering, topped off with the ultimate passive-aggressive triumph. When she says, "Some day you'll thank me for this," she is merely savoring a foretaste of the glory to come. Onward, Christian mothers.

A Delta mother has such meager pleasures that the world must conspire to make her life of sacrifice more tolerable. When we were on the old phone system and Central connected our calls, even Central tried to protect poor, deprived Mother. "Lida Jones," Central once fumed, "I am *not* going to put your call through. Your mama's bridge club hasn't finished their first rubber."

We don't know why Southern mothers suffer more than Yankee mothers, or even Midwestern mothers. But they do—and if they aren't suffering, they have a Yankee gene somewhere. It may be that, regardless of their daddy's income, all Southern mothers were brought up on the legend of their family's great wealth. So many Southerners believe that they used to be wealthy and that they "lost their money," that it makes you want to ask, "Where'd you put it, Miz Jones?" But that wouldn't be nice. Or it may just be that Southern mothers have the supremely daunting calling of turning heathen children into ladies and gentlemen. Or it may just be that suffering is noble, and our mothers are nothing if not noble.

You might think that mothers who aren't poor and have plenty of advantages would not be obligated to suffer. But you would be wrong. Even a mother who is waited on hand and foot is expected to suffer. It's not nice not to suffer. "I love my children," one pampered Southern mother sighed, "but they are so . . . [she searched for the right word] . . . so *daily*." She tried to make people think that she had actually changed their diapers, which everybody in town knew was a lie. To bolster the impression of unremitting toil, she often took a basket of peas to the doctor's office, where she would sit ostentatiously shelling them in the waiting room. The Southern writer Florence King once wrote that the more awful a lady's sufferings during "the change"—as we were brought up to say—the more aristocratic she is. If the change nearly sends you to Whitfield, the state insane asylum, then you are a lady. It is the same with motherhood. If you don't suffer, you aren't doing it right. "Ah worried and worried" is the Southern mother's favorite boast.

While suffering never gets boring, sometimes saying, "You're sending me to an early grave," over and over does. That is why the Southern mother must devise creative and interesting ways to convey this sentiment. When, for example, a Southern mother says, "I prayed to have a child for ten years, and then I had you," what she means is: "Why didn't I pray for a *polite* child?" A Southern daughter knows exactly what Mother means. When Mother is particularly aggrieved, she might pose at the front door and muse sadly, "I am going outside," adding poignantly, "I do not know if I shall return." She will. In a life spent among strangers, nobody would grasp the full import of her sacrifices. Now, that *would* be suffering.

Although our mothers are indestructible, we grew up believing that they were fragile and always on the verge of desperate remedy. "I'd jump off the bridge," they said, "but I'd have to stand in line." Presumably, the Mississippi River Bridge is so clogged with suffering Southern mothers that you can't jump spur-of-the-moment. Another mother, going through a divorce, found Sundays extremely difficult. With the family assembled, she frequently tearfully announced that she felt she had to end it all. She said she was going to "suicide," and she nearly drove her persnickety, prim daughter to doing just that by using a noun as a verb. "Well, Mama, how are you going to do it?" the daughter asked. "I am going to drive into the lake," she said. Southern mothers seem to go in for planning watery deaths, perhaps because the Delta used to be a swampland. "But, Mama," the daughter persisted, "you know you don't drive." "Ya-yes, I know," Mama replied. "I'll drink a glass of sherry first." She lived to be ninety, proving that getting it all out can be conducive to longevity.

We know one Southern mother who found a particularly inventive way to convey the terrible pangs of childbirth, which she had endured with well-bred stoicism. "Lower-class people can't stand the pain of childbirth," she would say, mentioning in passing that her mother-in-law, Velda Jane, for instance, who wasn't up to snuff, was the mother of only one child. Poor Velda Jane. Whatever her pain threshold, Velda Jane's failure to make the most of her child-bearing years may also have been the result of being widowed at the age of nineteen. Still, that was not the point. The point was that *somebody* had suffered. It killed two birds with one stone: Velda Jane was the other.

Sometimes a Southern martyr goes too far. We're afraid that Olivia Morgan once definitely overplayed the martyr hand. When Olivia was in the hospital once, she became convinced that she was going to die. She had been bored for days, and dying was actually an improvement on just lying in bed. Dying provided a drama, something all Southern mothers like. Olivia Morgan got on the phone. She called all her friends, relatives, and the rector of St. James. "Hello," she'd say, "this is Olivia Morgan, and if you want to see me alive, you should come right now. I just have this feeling that I am going to die tonight." She had quite a few visitors, and it was gratifying. They had to bring in extra chairs. Even her gruff brother came running over to bid farewell. But she did not die that night, perhaps because she'd had so much fun saying good-bye. The next morning, she had to get on the phone for a second round of announcements. "Hello, this is Olivia Morgan, and I'm not dead, but I'm just *dying* of embarrassment," she was forced to admit.

False starts at dying were a way of life for Miss Olivia's family. Her father stood daily at the dinner table and declared, as he sharpened his carving knife, that he was not long for this world. "Thirty days hence and I shall not be here," he always said. The "hence" was a special touch. When Alice Hunt, a visitor, piped up one day and said impishly, "Thirty days hath September, April, June, and John Gilliam," we thought for a split second that the carving knife wasn't going to be used on the roast beef. Mr. Gilliam quit dying for a few weeks, but eventually resumed this pleasurable activity. One time, when Olivia Morgan thought she might die, her daughters didn't know if she was posing or really dying. "She may be exaggerating," one said on the phone to an aunt, "but she hasn't wrapped her helmet do in toilet paper or applied her Swiss Performing lotion. That might mean she's really dying this time." Fortunately, it didn't; Olivia Morgan lived to die another day.

A story that always brought tears to the eyes of Olivia Gilliam Morgan's daughters was the traumatic saga of Olivia's near-death trip from Sewanee home to Greenville. Olivia Morgan, a young divorcee, and her eldest daughter had spent a few months in Sewanee, the Episcopal university in Tennessee. She had been "playing hostess," as it was called, for her brother, a faculty member. When Olivia got to the train depot, she realized she had only a few dollars left. A non-martyr might have said, "Can I borrow a few dollars?" A martyr sees other opportunities. "Ah spent all my money feeding Little Olivia," she would recall often in the ensuing years. It was during World War II, and Olivia Morgan was exposed to the sight of a woman nursing her baby in public. Olivia closed her eyes and wondered why she had been chosen for this living hell. The most heart-rending moment came when, as she felt death's imminence, Olivia held her child before her eyes and asked, in a trembling but courageous voice, "Little Olivia, recite your grandfather's address and telephone number."

At this point, Olivia Morgan's younger daughter, who had not been on this trip from hell, always felt tears welling up in her eyes. Until, that is, Aunt Adele, a latecomer to the family, asked, "Why didn't you just write a check, Olivia? You'd've been home before it got to the bank." Furthermore, she tactlessly pointed out that starving to death between Sewanee and Greenville is rare.

Martyrs may make you think they are weak, pitiful little things, strong only in the ability to suffer quietly. In fact, they are indomitable. Never cross a Southern martyr. Olivia Morgan would have done just fine in the covered wagon days. She would have beaten the Donners over the Donner Pass, without ruining her helmet hair or becoming a cannibal—as members of the Donner Party, alas, did. After all, she didn't own the proper fork with which to eat a human being.

'TIS THE SEASON TO . . . BE MARTYR, TRA LA LA LA LA LA LA LA LA

A SOUTHERN mother always remembers her childhood Christmases as among the happiest times of her life. She feels duty-bound to pass the joy along to the next generation. She sees the holidays as a time to shine, even if it just about kills her. Houses are overdone, and the groaning board may literally groan. She is determined to recapture the fairy tale of her own Christmases—of having a tree that hit the ceiling, stringing popcorn, and singing Christmas carols—and to impress her fellow mothers. Despite all the good intentions, Mama's preparations sometimes run amok. We remember one dear cousin who would go on a bender every time he sampled just one of Olivia Morgan's delicious rum balls. But there's always next year—and that (thank heavens!) is how traditions work. Rather than tethering us to the past, traditions help to guide us safely into the future. Here are some traditional Delta Christmas recipes.

Rum Balls

A charming but out-of-print cookbook, *Biscuits, Spoon Bread and Sweet Potatoes,* by Bill Neal, refers to rum balls as an indispensable part of every Southerner's Christmas, adding, "Also, some children feign inebriation after eating a couple of these." Unlike some more exotic ingredients, 'nillas are easy to get down here.

Ingredients
½ pound vanilla wafers
1 cup chopped nuts
2 tablespoons cocoa
1 cup Karo light corn syrup
¼ cup rum
Confectioners' sugar

Crush the vanilla wafers fine. Mix the crumbs with the nuts, cocoa, corn syrup, and rum until they form a firm paste. Dust the palms of your hands with sugar and shape into small balls (about 1 inch). Allow to dry for about an hour, then roll in more sugar. Store the rum balls in an airtight container for several hours. Just before serving, roll in sugar again.

Makes about thirty balls.

Wild Turkey—For Eating, Not Drinking

A staunch traditionalist, Ann Call always went through the ritual of preparing an unvarying menu for Thanksgiving. After Gayden married, Mrs. Call made one change: Instead of a store-bought turkey that had a pop-up button, they always had a wild turkey that had been killed by Gayden's intrepid husband. The thermometer is such a convenience, but the wild turkey is much more delicious. Lord knows what you have to go through to kill one. But it's worth it, enough so to make Ann Call vary a Thanksgiving recipe that had been used in the family for a hundred years, even before we had the help of a thermometer to aid us. We kid you not!

Rinse the bird and remove all the errant fuzz. Pat dry. Salt and pepper inside and out, and rub with butter (inside and out). Stuff with onion, celery, and/or fruit. If put in foil—open the foil after the bird has cooked up to the last hour. Then baste the bird several times during the last hour of cooking. Cooking times:

10 to 12 pounds 400° (2½ to 3 hours)
14 to 16 pounds 400° (3 to 3½ hours)
18 to 20 pounds 400° (3¼ to 3½ hours)

DRESSING

*A*nn Call made two pans of dressing, one with oysters, one without. Her mantra was "Never stuff a wild turkey." Also, never stuff a domestic turkey with oyster dressing. Oyster dressing must always be baked in a separate pan. The corn bread should be made the day before. A rich, homemade chicken stock is, always, a good thing to have on hand. You can freeze it, so there really is no excuse not to have some around at all times. A well-flavored chicken stock makes a big difference in the final product.

.   .   .

Ingredients
2 cups chopped celery
2 chopped bell peppers
3 cups chopped yellow onions
6 green onions, sliced (some green tops)
2 cloves garlic, minced
1 stick unsalted butter
1/2 cup chopped parsley
1 teaspoon dried thyme
1 teaspoon dried sage
Salt and freshly ground black pepper to taste
Dash of Tabasco
10 cups crumbled real corn bread baked in a black iron skillet

6 cups toasted bread cubes, preferably made from old French bread
3 cups homemade chicken stock
3 eggs, beaten
6 hard-boiled eggs, peeled and chopped (not too finely)
1 cup chopped pecans
Turkey giblets, boiled and chopped (optional)
1 pint raw oysters (optional)

Sauté the celery, bell peppers, onions, and garlic in the butter (as needed).

Mix in the remaining herbs and seasonings.

Soak the breads in chicken stock and add any remaining butter (melted). In a large pan, mix the vegetables and breads.

Add the beaten eggs. Gently add the chopped eggs, pecans, and giblets. Correct the seasoning if needed and then separate the dressing into two pans.

If using oysters, drain and reserve the juice. Sauté the oysters briefly until the edges curl. Add to the dressing and moisten if necessary with the reserved oyster juice.

Bake in a greased pan, uncovered, at 375° for one hour or until firm.

Yield depends on how big a turkey your husband shoots.

Eggnog

When we learned to drink: age five. No Southern Christmas is complete without eggnog. The milk-and-alcohol combination was popular in Europe and it came to the United States with the earliest colonists. It's a good drink for toasting the health of family and friends.

.   .   .

Ingredients
1 dozen eggs, separated (save the whites)
1/2 pound confectioners' sugar
1 cup good bourbon
1/2 cup good brandy
1 quart whipping cream, whipped
1 quart half-and-half
Freshly grated nutmeg

Beat the egg yolks, adding the sugar gradually. Add the bourbon and brandy a little at the time and beat until incorporated. Refrigerate overnight.

Fold the whipped cream into this mixture and add the half-and-half until the desired thickness is reached. Whip the egg whites until stiff and fold in. Garnish with freshly grated nutmeg.

Makes twelve punch cups.

TaTa's Cheese Rolls

*L*ong before the advent of designer cheeses, Mrs. Call's kitchen helper, TaTa, made this wonderful cheese roll. Gayden swears they had it with the eggnog. Believe it or not, they are an excellent accompaniment. They also go nicely with hard liquor—and, frankly, they are stronger than the booze. I just found the recipe and made it. It's as good as I remember.

. . .

Ingredients
1 pound extra sharp Cheddar cheese, grated
6 ounces Philadelphia Cream Cheese
5 cloves of garlic, minced
Tabasco
Paprika
Chili powder

Mix the grated cheese and the cream cheese in the bowl of a food processor. Add the garlic and process until blended. Add several good shakes of Tabasco. Make two logs and roll in a combination of paprika and chili powder. Wrap individually in Saran Wrap and chill. TaTa never used a food processor; she grated the cheese, minced the garlic, and mixed all by hand, kneading until all was well incorporated. Works perfectly.

Makes 2 ten-inch rolls.

The Best Tomato Aspic

We can't write a cookbook without aspic. This is an aspic served every Christmas. It's very clear and red and green, topped with a special low-cal blend of homemade mayonnaise and cream cheese. And anyway, calories don't count at Christmas.

*   *   *

Ingredients
12 cups tomato juice
10 packets unflavored gelatin
3 cucumbers, peeled
3 tomatoes, peeled
1 clove garlic, peeled
1 large onion
2 carrots, peeled and chopped
14 green onion stems, chopped
1 large green pepper, chopped
2 stalks celery, chopped
2 teaspoons salt
1 teaspoon Lawry's Seasoned Salt
2 teaspoons white pepper
2 teaspoons Tabasco

2 teaspoons Lea & Perrins Worcestershire Sauce
3/4 cup olive oil
1/4 cup lemon juice

In a very large pan (the size you would use to make soup), heat 6 cups of the tomato juice. Sprinkle the gelatin over the top and stir after each addition. Cook over low heat until the gelatin has dissolved.

Meanwhile, in a food processor pulse the cucumbers, tomatoes, garlic clove, and onion. Add this mixture to the gelatin/tomato juice mixture. Add the additional 6 cups of tomato juice and the balance of the chopped vegetables and the seasonings and the oil and lemon juice. Fill 2 Bundt pans and refrigerate until firm. Overnight is perfect.

Makes enough to fill 2 ten-cup Bundt pans.

TOPPING

Ingredients
1 cup homemade mayonnaise
8 ounces cream cheese

Blend in a food processor. Use as you would mayo alone. Sometimes Mother would simply use sour cream as a topping, but we all preferred the version with the most calories possible.

Dove and Oyster Pie

*D*elta men spend a lot of time hunting. Dove season is always enjoyed, and inevitably there is a package of dove breasts in the freezer. In the cooler months, combined with oysters, another cold-weather treat, this is a perfect main dish . . . clearing out the freezer for Christmas.

Ingredients
12 dove breasts, filleted
1 large onion, sliced
2 stalks celery, sliced
2 bay leaves
6 peppercorns
Salt
Pastry for a double-crust pie (cream cheese pastry is excellent)
1 pint oysters, drained and patted dry
White pepper
2 tablespoons flour
1/2 cup minced parsley
Dash of Lea & Perrins Worcestershire Sauce
Dash of Tabasco
6 tablespoons unsalted butter

Cover the dove breasts with water. Add the onion, celery, bay leaves, and peppercorns. Bring to a boil. Lower heat, cover, and simmer until the dove breasts are cooked and tender. Add salt to the broth and cool the dove breasts in the broth. Butter a very deep pie dish or casserole and line with pie pastry. Drain the dove breasts, reserving the stock. Place in the pastry and add the oysters, scattering them evenly among the dove breasts.

Salt and pepper generously. Combine two cups of the reserved dove stock and the two tablespoons flour. Be sure there are no lumps. Add the minced parsley and a dash of Lea & Perrins and Tabasco. Pour over the dove breasts and oysters. Dot this with 4 tablespoons of the butter. Cover with the remaining crust. Dot the crust with the remaining two tablespoons butter.

Bake at 350° for 45 minutes.

Serves eight.

Charlotte Russe

*T*his is beautiful made in a cut-glass bowl and brought to the table to be served by the lady of the house. There are some who use a springform pan. Either way it is delicious, and a Southern sine qua non. Of course, some of us call it Charlotte Roush. You know—like the Roushian Empire headed by Catherine the Great. But you don't have to pronounce it right to enjoy it. We love to serve it on Christmas Day.

.   .   .

Ingredients
2 packages unflavored gelatin
1/2 cup cold water
2 eggs, beaten
2 cups whole milk, scalded
Pinch of salt
1/2 cup sugar
1 teaspoon vanilla
1/2 cup sherry (Dry Sack preferred)
4 cups whipping cream
2 packages ladyfingers

Soften the gelatin in water. Using the eggs, milk, salt, and sugar, make the custard. Add the gelatin. When slightly cooled, add the vanilla and sherry. Refrigerate until thickened. Whip the cream and fold into the custard. Line your serving dish with the ladyfingers and pour in the mixture. Chill until set.

Serves ten to twelve.

Ambrosia

*A*mbrosia, food of the gods, is a Christmas dinner finale, usually accompanied by a slice of nut cake or fruitcake. Like many Delta mothers, Charlotte's mother, Julia Morgan Hays, liked to serve the dessert plates from a table by her chair at her father's dining table. Coffee in demitasse cups added to the festive atmosphere—and all Southern females love to "pour."

You cannot have Christmas in the Delta without ambrosia. It's against the law. There are two types of Delta cook: the purist and the permissive. This elixir in its purist form consists of *fresh* coconut and *fresh* oranges, with sugar, layered. Purists refuse to put cherries on top of the ambrosia—so tacky! As even the purest Delta cooks acquire grandchildren, however, cherries sometimes make their way into the ambrosia. Children love the sight of bright cherries on their ambrosia. But even grandchildren don't make tiny marshmallows acceptable! Ambrosia is actually an adult taste, and children like it more if there are enhancements. Some recipes call for a dash of pineapple juice, sherry, or Grand Marnier. A fatigued martyr may need it!

. . .

Ingredients (for the purists)
8 large seedless oranges
¼ cup sugar
1 small coconut

Peel the oranges, being careful to remove *all* the pith. Layer the orange sections, which have been cut into thin slices, with a sprinkling of sugar and a sprinkling of fresh coconut, shredded. Repeat this process until you reach the top of the bowl. Add a hefty layer of grated fresh coconut.

This must be refrigerated for four to six hours. A beautiful end to a perfect Christmas dinner.

Serves twelve, frugally.

Aunt Evelyn's Tipsy Pudding

*G*eorge Washington, a fellow Southerner even if he never slept in the Delta, loved trifle—and so do we. Tipsy pudding is another name for trifle. You'll feel so much better after a few servings! This recipe is from Charlotte's late aunt Evelyn Hall from Bourbon, Mississippi. It was given to us by Emily Griffith, Aunt Evelyn's daughter.

.   .   .

CUSTARD

Ingredients
2 eggs
¼ cup sugar
Pinch of salt
2 cups milk, scalded
2 tablespoons flour
Cold milk
½ teaspoon vanilla

Beat the eggs slightly, add the sugar and salt, and stir the scalded milk in gradually. Place in a double boiler, stirring constantly. Add the flour dissolved in a little cold milk. Continue to stir until the mixture thickens. Add the vanilla, and set aside to cool. It can be made ahead of time and put in the refrigerator.

PUDDING

Ingredients
2¹/₂ dozen ladyfingers
Bourbon
²/₃ cup chopped pecans
1 pint whipping cream, whipped

Put a layer of the ladyfingers (or you can use broken-up pieces of pound cake) in a bowl, sprinkle with bourbon, spoon in the custard, and sprinkle with pecans. Add another layer and repeat until bowl is filled. Put the whipped cream on top. Place in refrigerator overnight.

Serves eight.

Coffee Cake

*C*hristmas Day isn't a day for a big Delta breakfast with grits and bacon and all the heart-healthy fixin's. Coffee cake is perfect to tide you over until the main meal is served. This is another recipe from Evelyn Hall.

. . .

Ingredients
1 cup butter (Aunt Evelyn used 1 stick butter
  and 1 stick margarine, combined)
2 cups sugar
2 eggs
2 cups sifted cake flour
1 teaspoon baking powder
¼ teaspoon salt
1 cup sour cream
½ teaspoon vanilla

Cream the butter and sugar, add the eggs (after beating), add the dry ingredients, and mix. Add the sour cream and vanilla. Mix. Put half of the resulting batter in a cake pan. Add half of the topping (see below). Put in the rest of the batter, then the rest of the topping. Bake at 350° for 55 to 60 minutes. Cool and remove from pan.

TOPPING

Ingredients
½ cup chopped pecans
½ teaspoon cinnamon
2 tablespoons sugar

Mix all ingredients together.

Aunt Evelyn's Cream Puffs

*W*e seem to be on an Evelyn Hall run—but that's because she was such a great cook. Cream puffs are festive anytime, and they are especially nice at Christmas.

.   .   .

Ingredients
½ cup butter (1 stick)
1 cup boiling water
1 cup flour
4 eggs

Put the butter in a saucepan with the boiling water. Bring back to a boil, boiling until the butter is thoroughly melted. Add the flour all at once. Stir vigorously! Cook until the mixture is thick and smooth and does not stick to the side of the pan. Stir constantly so it won't burn. Remove, let cool. Add the eggs one at a time and beat thoroughly each time. Beat mixture well. Drop by spoonfuls on a greased baking sheet, 1½ inches apart. Bake at 400°. When the cream puffs are lightly browned, remove from the oven and slit the tops to release the steam so that the insides will not be gummy. About 35 minutes.

CREAM PUFF FILLING

Ingredients
6 tablespoons flour
1 cup sugar
⅛ teaspoon salt
3 cups milk, scalded
4 eggs (beaten)
2 teaspoons vanilla

Mix the dry ingredients together. Put the milk in a double boiler and scald. Add the dry ingredients to the milk, stirring constantly. Cook until smooth. Pour over the beaten eggs, stirring constantly. Return to the boiler and cook 10 minutes. Add the vanilla, and let cool in the refrigerator until you're ready to fill the puffs.

Makes ten, if petite.

Toasted Coconut Cake

"The best of all Southern cakes is the coconut cake," says our friend Linda Rogers Weiss of Greenville, South Carolina, a cookbook author and a member of the James Beard Foundation and the Southern Foodways Alliance. Linda was asked to create a recipe for a winter feature in a magazine—and this is the scrumptious result. "My thoughts turned to my mother's ambrosia," Linda recalled, "and how we were going to miss her terribly that coming Christmas. And, my other thought was—'How in the heck am I going to create a new coconut cake?' Every family in the South already has one. Or more. So, I walked around my kitchen with my hands on my hips, thinking that I was really going to mess this one up, and I had bitten off more than I could chew, when I noticed a jar of pineapple preserves in my pantry. And then the rest just came to me. It would be an ambrosia cake."

· · ·

CAKE

Ingredients
1½ sticks unsalted butter, room temperature
1½ cups sugar

½ cup pineapple preserves
4 large eggs
3 cups self-rising flour
1 cup sour cream
1 teaspoon vanilla

Preheat oven to 325°. Grease and flour (I use a baking spray) 4 9-inch cake pans. With an electric mixer, beat the butter, sugar, and pineapple preserves until light and fluffy. Add the eggs one at a time to the sugar mixture. Add alternately the flour and the sour cream, ending with the flour. Add the vanilla, and beat on high speed for 2 minutes. Distribute the batter evenly between the 4 pans.

Bake for 20 to 25 minutes or until a cake tester comes out clean. Remove from the oven. After 10 minutes, remove the cakes from the pans to a rack to cool. Then frost with the icing below.

Note: To make cupcakes, use an ice cream scoop and place the batter into 2½-inch paper cupcake cups. Bake for approximately 20 minutes or until done. Remove the cupcakes to a rack to cool.

FROSTING

Ingredients
1 package (8 ounces) coconut, toasted
1½ sticks unsalted butter, softened
1½ containers (8 ounces each) mascarpone cheese or 1½ packages
  (8 ounces each) cream cheese

1¹/₂ pounds confectioners' sugar
3 teaspoons coconut extract

Place the coconut on a cookie sheet and put into a 350° oven. Watch carefully and stir often until the coconut is lightly browned. Remove from the oven and set aside to cool.

Mix the butter and the mascarpone or cream cheese in a mixer with a wire whisk until creamy. Add the confectioners' sugar and the coconut extract. Mix until the sugar is well blended into the butter-and-cheese mixture.

Spread the frosting between the layers of the cake, along with a little of the toasted coconut. Spread frosting on the top and sides of the assembled cake. Using your hand like a cup, place the toasted coconut on the sides and top of the cake. Refrigerate. Bring the cake to room temperature before serving.

Note: Linda used the organic dried large-flaked coconut available at Whole Foods. If this coconut is not available, just use Baker's Angel Flake coconut, and either toast it, or just use it like it is.

Sweet Potato Casserole

*T*his is a Thanksgiving staple. Sometimes it appears in orange shells, other times in a Pyrex dish that slips into a silver holder. As children, we thought it was more like a dessert than a dinner dish. That must be why we liked it so much!

.　　.　　.

Ingredients
5 large sweet potatoes
1/2 cup sugar
1/2 cup unsalted butter
2 eggs, well beaten
1 to 1 1/2 teaspoons vanilla flavoring
2 teaspoons finely grated orange peel
1/4 cup whole milk or cream
1/4 cup bourbon or brandy
Dash of salt

Bake or boil the sweet potatoes and then mash.
    Add the balance of the ingredients.
    Taste and correct the seasoning.
    Put in a lightly greased baking dish.

TOPPING

Ingredients
⅓ cup melted butter
1 cup packed brown sugar
½ cup flour
1 cup chopped pecans

Melt the butter and add the balance of the ingredients.

Cover the top of the sweet potatoes.

Bake 30 minutes in a preheated 350° oven or until the topping is golden brown and the casserole is good and bubbly.

Serves twelve.

Sacrificial Lamb

*C*hristmas isn't the only season Mother runs herself ragged. There is also Easter (and any other holiday that comes to mind). This lamb recipe, which comes from our dear friend Bland Currie, is perfect for Easter lunch.

· · ·

LAMB MARINADE

Ingredients
2/3 inch chunk of fresh ginger
3/4 clove fresh garlic
1 medium yellow onion
1/4 cup red wine vinegar
1 1/2 cups olive oil
1 teaspoon salt
2/3 teaspoon freshly ground black pepper
1 handful fresh thyme

Bland says: "This is basically a vinaigrette for a leg of lamb. If you cannot get the fresh ingredients, do this another day because the recipe needs the freshest of ingredients to be a success. Put the ginger, garlic, onion, and vinegar in the bowl of the Cuisinart and process until it makes a paste. Slowly add the olive oil and the salt and pepper. Taste, taste, and taste. You may need more of an ingredient. Pour the marinade over the thyme and mix well."

Coat a butterflied leg of lamb with the marinade and wrap it in plastic wrap. Put it in the icebox overnight or for several hours. Bring the lamb to room temperature and scrape off the marinade. If you grill this over a real charcoal fire until it is medium rare it will be as good as lamb ever is, and do not forget to let it rest for 10 or 15 minutes before it is sliced. Otherwise, cook it in a 350° oven until it is medium rare.

One 6–7 pound leg of lamb serves eight.

The Relish Tray

W e love to have a relish tray of savory treats on holidays. It is passed during the main course and may include pickled peaches, bread-and-butter pickles, and other goodies to embellish the menu. Frances Shackelford's mother, Mrs. Sam Wilson of Montrose, Arkansas, always had candied grapefruit or orange rinds on her relish tray. Here is that recipe:

. . .

Ingredients

Grapefruit rinds, cut in 1/2-inch strips,
  or orange peels, cut in 1/4-inch strips
  with all the white removed
1 cup sugar
1 cup water
Beaten egg whites

Peel the fruit using a very sharp vegetable peeler, leaving all the white part behind. Cut into long strips. Bring the water and sugar to a boil and add the strips. Bring back to a boil and immediately put the strips in their syrup in the icebox for three days. Afterward, they may be drained and stored in an airtight container.

Before you're ready to serve them, dip the peels in egg whites, coat with sugar, and put on a rack to dry. (Some people are skittish about raw egg whites—but they taste great!)

These are also lovely served alongside chocolate or citrus desserts. It looks as though you have worked really hard.

Egg Salad Sandwich

*F*or some reason, little egg sandwiches are springlike. We never seem to have had them in the dark ages (Lent), but they began to appear around Easter. This egg salad is generally spread on whole wheat or rye (and not on the delicious white, killer marshmallow bread of the fifties and sixties—but don't worry, that'll probably make a comeback, as eggs did!).

The secret of a good egg salad is to use homemade mayonnaise and not too much of it. You do not want a soggy product.

.   .   .

Ingredients (for the purist)
Hard-boiled eggs
Homemade mayonnaise
Chopped celery
Chopped green onions
Salt and pepper

Combine, cover, and chill.

Additions (for the not so pure, as always to taste)
Capers
Curry powder
Chives
Grated lemon rind
Cream cheese

Mrs. Fritz Schas's Chocolate Sauce

A Memphian with deep Delta roots, Mrs. Schas created an atmosphere in her Goodlett Street house that is fondly recalled by her children's legions of friends (including Charlotte!). Everything that came from the Schas kitchen was delicious. This chocolate sauce makes ice cream an elegant dessert—any dinner can become a holiday dinner.

*   *   *

Ingredients
1 stick butter
8 Tablespoons sugar
8 Tablespoons Droste Dutch cocoa (or some good, dark cocoa)
16 ounces Hershey's Syrup

Heat the butter, sugar, and cocoa until dissolved. Add the Hershey's chocolate syrup. Bring to a low simmer and continue to barely simmer for about 5 minutes. The sauce thickens when put over ice cream. The longer you heat it the more it thickens, so you can try different lengths of cooking time. For added festivity: a dash of brandy at the last minute.

Makes approximately one and a half cups.

Mrs. Schas's Date Pudding

This is another dessert festive enough for a holiday
meal but good at any time.

· · ·

Ingredients

1 cup flour

2 tablespoons baking powder

1 pound pecans, shelled and chopped

2 packages chopped dates

4 eggs, separated

1 cup sugar

1 teaspoon vanilla

1 pinch salt

Whipped cream

Sift flour and baking powder together. Sift over the chopped
nuts and dates. Beat yolks well. Add sugar to the yolks and beat
until smooth. Add vanilla and salt and, lastly, fold in well-beaten
egg whites. Bake in slow oven about an hour. Cut into squares
and serve with whipped cream.

A GARLAND OF SOUTHERN LADIES, THORNS AND ALL

What are the two strongest forces in any small Southern town? Why, the DAR and the garden clubs, of course. Greenville has eight garden clubs. As we pondered our flower fixation, we suddenly realized that the best way to explain the types of lady in the Delta is . . . by comparing each to a flower.

We hope we won't make anybody prickly, but here goes:

Black-eyed Susan: Gets rowdy after a few cocktails. Will do damage to another woman or man. Daughters' friends think she is a hoot. Daughters, not so much.

Boll Weevil: Not a flower, but a pest known throughout the South, she can burn through an entire family fortune in one season . . . avoid at all costs. Her daughters find it is a good idea if they embrace being shabby genteel, because it sounds better than just plain po'. Which is what Mama Boll Weevil made them.

Camellia: A combat or commando . . . a titanium steel magnolia. When times get tough, she shines. "Beauty under adversity." Adversity is somebody

Continued

trying to take an honor from one of her precious baby camellias.

Chrysanthemum: Collects Tiffany silver; a big-ticket girl, marries a good provider. Daughters are very much like Mama. Won't fall in love with the football hero, unless his daddy is a financial hero.

Day Lily: A modest, demure lady, runs the library and is pious until the cocktail hour . . . Her dangerous cousin is **Tiger Lily**, a woman who would kill for her family. They compete through their daughters. Unfortunately, TL's daughter is a Phi Beta Kappa, which doesn't count in the Delta. Day Lily wins, even though she had to send daughter **Wild Ginger** to convent school (where bad or intellectually uninspired Protestant girls go, if Daddy can conquer the fear that they will become nuns).

Easter Lily: A pious St. James dowager. You thought she was contemplating the spiritual realm until you noticed that she always sat by the big stained glass window given by the Lily family—to the glory of God, and the Lily family, too. Will withdraw her support if daughter can't be state regent of the Children of the American Revolution.

Continued

Iris, bearded: Aunt Iris may suffer from a hormone imbalance. She is best described as a "handsome woman." Inherited her family tractor franchise and runs it better than any man. She can change a tire without using tools and uncorks wine bottles with her teeth. But she is not a mother. Mother insists that Aunt was once in love with *a man* from Inverness—but we know this isn't true. And we are so fond of her special friend, Aunt Pearl.

Ivy: A clingy mother, she is permanently attached at the hip to Baby Darling, whose room at Ole Miss she decorates. Baby Darling's shrink has come to loathe her. But Baby Darling can't make the break.

Lily of the Valley: If Mother is a virgin, how did she have children? Lily is even more hesitant than other Delta mothers to share the "facts of life" with her six daughters. But they know anyway—and how!

Magnolia: A moonlight-on-the-Delta belle, this mother is always disappointed by rebellious daughters. They read big thick books and want to talk about current events. How boring. Mother retaliates by calling all her daughters' friends to talk about boyfriends, cruelly hinting that her daughters don't have any.

Continued

Marigold: Marry Gold—get it? A gold digger of legendary status. Not a mother. Children would ruin her figure.

Narcissus: Slightly self-involved, Narcissa is a third-generation Chi Omega, never seen without a compact. When another girl nearly beat Little Narcissa in the race for the title of Miss Hospitality, Big Narcissa briefly considered taking out a contract. But the other girl didn't do well on the charm questions. (Yes, Miss Hospitality is a real, statewide title.)

Petunia: A bit chubby, well liked by all but not thought of in romantic terms, she married a CPA and secretly encourages Little Petunia to be racy. History must not repeat itself.

Poison Ivy: A man trap in her heyday, she is always urging her daughters to steal their girlfriends' beaux. Daughters can't decide which is worse—the mean advice or calling them beaux.

Poppy: She likes booze and sedatives, so her daughters retaliate by joining the Presbyterian Church and becoming teetotalers.

Queen Anne's Lace: A tiny, fussy, now elderly and doily-obsessed older lady, she still wears gloves for

Continued

her afternoon walk. A maiden lady English teacher, she has no children of her own but is beloved by nieces and students.

Rose: She is lovely to the eye, but watch for her thorns. The other flowers do not cross her. She can be a climber. Little Rose is just as bad as Big Rose—sometimes we wish they were yellow roses, but they aren't.

Rosemary: Always in the kitchen because she has so many chillun and menfolk to feed. Rosemary was not expected to become an earth mother during her raucous career at the SAE fraternity house.

Strangler Fig: She mothers her family to death. She'll dab a hanky with spit to clean her children's faces the way a lioness licks its cubs. Refuses to let her children grow up.

Sugar Snap: Calls everybody "sugah." Everybody is Miz Darling or Miz Precious. "Isn't that just sweet?" she says, making you hope you can make it to the powder room. You can get diabetes from one of her thank-you notes, which you'll receive if you so much as smile at her at St. James, which she has practically taken over after rejecting Methodism. Beneath the

Continued

froth is ice. Clawed her way into the garden club, but her daughters are really sweet. This time it's the son who is in therapy—long-term.

Planting Instructions

Annual: Lifespan of a mistress. A homey gal who'd love to have children of her own. In fact, she does—and, now that you mention it, doesn't he look a little bit like Mr. . . . ?

Biennial: A second wife. She gets a new car, fur, jewels the first year. Face-lift every two years. No children of her own, and it kills her to have to be nice to the steps. But that won't last forever. She has already started plotting against them.

Perennial: In for the long haul. One marriage, one house, one hairstyle. The first wife, the only wife.

Our thanks to Dickson Miller for this list.

CHAPTER VI

❧

Grande Dames and Other Mothers: No Matter What Kind of Southern Mother You Had, Your Therapist Can Help You Work Through It

ONE OF the most annoying of Southern mothers is the one who sits at the bridge table condemning the children of other mothers. "I'm so thankful that Precious would never do anything like that," she says, all too often. When Precious is arrested for playing strip poker at the Seven Oaks bar, supercilious Mother throws a hissy fit—and then forbids anybody ever to mention Precious's transgression again. It hardly matters, as this mishap will almost certainly pale in comparison to the next.

Flamboyant mothers who make dramatic entrances at parties

produce daughters who desire to follow in their stiletto footsteps. "I want people to love me for my mind, not my body," announces Flamboyant Mother's daughter, who has just stepped into the Greenville Country Club's Sunday lunch clad in the same skimpy evening gown she was wearing last night when the police officers stopped her for speeding. But she wants them to at least *notice* her body.

There's the mother who was once famed throughout the Delta for her beauty and who says things like "Why does Precious need to go to college? She's going to get married, isn't she?" Precious obliges by getting married—frequently. The very dissimilar DAR mother, not the most forward-looking of parents, hastens to enroll her Precious in CAR (Children of the American Revolution) at birth. Mama is secretly proud that Precious is famous in CAR circles for her daring paper "Tom Paine, Radical," which Mama found brilliant—even if its politically advanced sentiments nearly sent Mrs. Worthington, the state regent, to the Delta Medical Center. But Mother is misguided—brains are not the source of Precious's fame. Precious is known throughout the state as "the CAR loose leg." What with those humongous, medal-ready bosoms, Precious is likely to end up as state regent herself one day, despite her reputation.

Pushy Mother—or Alpha Mother—drives everybody crazy going on and on about Precious's charm and virtues, and just to ensure that Precious's charm doesn't go to waste on the socially inferior, she has fought her way into the garden club. After a few years of weeding her prized camellias, she comes to believe she founded the garden club. Pushy Mother sends gifts and food offerings to all the socially prominent matrons, who worry that they'll get diarrhea from her casseroles. Oddly enough, Precious turns out fine, marries well—and moves away. She always tries to remember that Mama meant well.

Sometimes, it must be said, the Alpha Mother was just trying to be nice, but she has offended so many people with her pushiness that she is always suspected of social climbing—and is often guilty as charged. One Mrs. Alpha, for example, always trolled the St. James bulletin, which included names of prominent parishioners who were celebrating a birthday. She showed up with a stuffed animal for Mr. Everard, who, instead of realizing she had confused his namesake grandson's birthday for his, thought she was alluding to his second childhood. He never forgave her. In her eagerness, Alpha Mother is always making mistakes of this sort. We'll never forget when one Alpha Mother invited her nieces and sister-in-law to a nice lunch at the country club. It was Good Friday, but Mrs. Alpha couldn't take a chance—her niece's prominent friend might not be available on Monday. Sister-in-law was scandalized at being invited out on a sacred day—and she said so repeatedly—right after she got back from lunch at the country club.

Another overpowering mother, the third-generation Chi Omega, often turns into the sweetie-pie-darling-aren't-you-cute mother, who may or may not be as sweet as she seems. If she stabs you in the back while thumping her Bible, that can be a sign that she is not genuine. She is akin to but not quite the same as the loving-hands-at-home mother, who has already been described as putting so much starch in her daughter's petticoat that the loving-hands-at-home daughter looks like Scarlett O'Hara on steroids and can't sit down normally, lest her skirt fly up, revealing elaborately monogrammed eyelet panties. She always has a homemade treat ready for after school. Nothing says loving (or smothering) like something from the loving-hands-at-home mother. Too bad Precious retaliates by refusing to learn how to boil water.

Miz Darling, another variant of the notorious Alpha Mother, shops at Pappagallo in Memphis, where everything can color coordinate, or at best match with everything else in her wardrobe. She dresses her children in matching outfits; they look like the Von Trapp family from *The Sound of Music*. If she is Baptist, her daughter's spend-the-night guests are awakened to the sound of her at the piano, belting out all the verses of "Sweet Hour of Prayer." Does Precious rebel? No, she grows up to be just like Miz Darling.

The Delta boasts quite a few mothers who might best be described as Donna Reed aspirants. These strive for Betty Crocker perfection. Plastic see-through slipcovers cocoon every item in the house, even her husband. She likes to serve pot roast TV dinners. She has possibly spent time in the state mental hospital. She had a heck of a time deciding whether to name her daughter Meriwether or Killi, and finally went with Wendi.

The Southern mother is often so besotted with Precious that she can't see her as others perhaps do. "Isn't Precious beautiful?"

asked Mrs. Dabney, one such mother, as Precious flailed about on the dance floor. "Yes, if you like an elephant in a tutu," replied old Mrs. Sutter, who had had a few. Mrs. Dabney didn't hear exactly what the old dear said, but nevertheless cut her from her Christmas card list. Precious, endowed with supreme self-confidence, married several well-to-do husbands. She regards herself as the most beautiful woman in Weight Watchers.

Perhaps the trickiest of Southern mothers is the grande dame. She is a hard act to follow, even though she plays her role with seeming effortlessness. Grande dames are so exalted that every community can have only one or two at a time. She may have gone to school in Virginia and is either obviously goal-directed—the garden club presidency is an appropriate outlet for her talents—or is so vague that her goal is not to get lost on the way to the grocery. The latter type is likely to muse, when the weather is cold, "Why aren't the other ladies wearing their furs?" The grande dame is often not a snob, which means it is sometimes frustrating to get her to blackball trashy people from the garden club. She is more than willing, however, to mislay their invitations on the way to the post office, which is so much nicer than voting against them. Her customary curse word is "horse feathers."

A favorite afternoon topic of conversation among our Ladies Who Cocktail—the Delta variant of Ladies Who Lunch—is: Who are the reigning grande dames today? It is never hard to reach consensus. We know who they are—as do their daughters. The daughter of a grande dame has an important life decision to make: join them, or drive them crazy. Alas, many choose the latter option. One of our favorite grande dame daughters was once spotted selling flowers on Bourbon Street, the very same street on which she sang the blues in a nightclub. Others, perhaps more sensibly, just join the board of the Debutante Club and let fate take its course—if it is intended that they will one day emerge as grande dames, so be it; if not, they are still unwilling to join an ashram or sing on Bourbon Street.

Closely related to the grande dame is the racy grande dame, who would be a grande dame herself, if she could resist the siren call of eccentricity. Mrs. Robert Shaw, who enjoyed being driven around town so that her townspeople could view her latest turban, was one. (It must in addition be said that Mrs. Shaw also enjoyed being chauffeured around her own backyard in her turban to see if her flower beds needed weeding, a task she would have delegated.) She had begun her march toward being a racy grande dame early, when as a girl she decided, out of nowhere, that she was destined for operatic greatness. Instead of going to the Met, she stayed home, where it became de rigueur, as she might have put it, to have her sing at weddings. If the future Mrs. Robert Shaw didn't sing at your wedding, you weren't married. As a full-fledged racy grande dame, Mrs. Robert Shaw made it a habit to get under her bed and eat Red Hot candies at the same time every day. Being a racy grande dame requires a level of courage and creativity not granted to everybody. She is often best friends with the grande dame, who, with a tinge of envy (it's hard to be perfect all the time), recognizes her as an edgy version of herself. As a mother the racy grande dame is strenuous; her daughter typically tries to live up to Mother's high standards.

The Intellectual Mother is the Delta's most problematical. She is often unkempt, and may say things that are offensive. "Isn't Betsy Jones the most boring person in Washington County?" Intellectual Mother will say to somebody who has just asked Betsy Jones to serve as godmother to Baby Girl or Beau Jr. Intellectual Mother delights in making Aunt Isabel take her coffee beneath the Martin Luther King poster. She offers her daughter an option: How about a trip to Europe instead of making your debut? Daughter, being thoroughly tired of being the child of a freak, inevitably opts for making her debut, much to Intellectual Mother's horror—or, as she puts it, chagrin. We would say that the Intellectual Mother often goes in for being eccentric—if that weren't redundant. One of our favorite Intellectual Mothers used to drive around the Delta picking up Co-cola bottles on the side of the highway. She returned them for the deposit, which she saved up for trips to Europe (Intellectual Mothers love Europe). Why she didn't just ask her husband for the trip, like a normal mother, we don't know.

As you can see, all our mothers are lots of fun—but the Party Mother is the most fun of all— unless, of course, you are trying to do your homework. Homework. Isn't that what ugly girls do? Come gossip with Mother—that's more fun. No matter when Lavinia Highsmith, one of our favorite party mothers, came home from evenings out, she always got on the intercom. "Calling all dancing bears," she would sing out, "calling all dancing bears." This was the signal for Lavinia's children, who had been up in the bed, as we like to say, to get up out of the bed and do what children were put on earth by God to do: entertain Party Mother's friends. Daughters of Party Mothers can make a mean martini at an age when most of us are still stealing from our parents' liquor cabinet. And does this mean that daughters of Party Mothers—exhausted before their time—grow up to be sticks in the Mississippi mud? Not hardly, as we like to say down here. The daughters of Party Mothers are the girls most likely to dance on tables at various Delta honky-tonks, dancing on tables being the secret ambition of every Delta girl. It helps if you started out as a dancing bear.

Then there is the Flapper Mother, alternately known as the ageless belle mother or teen angel mother. "I am Alice Hunt, and I am the adult child of a teenager," Alice Hunt used to announce in her DSM 12-step group. She did not mean Mrs. Hunt was literally a teenage mother—in fact, Mrs. Hunt was forty when Alice was born. She was a teenager at heart, though. "I don't feel a day older than when all the boys wanted to dance with me," Mrs. Hunt often observed. She didn't always act older, either, Alice sometimes felt like noting. It was, after all, Mrs. Hunt, not Alice Hunt, who was deeply (and ecstatically) aware that of all the girls in her senior class only Alice had been enrolled long enough to meet the requirement to be May Day Queen. Alice Hunt would have died before being May Day Queen. The school apparently felt the same way; confronted with the specter of Alice Hunt, famous primarily for not being able to figure out that Noxzema wasn't shampoo, as May Day Queen, it changed the rules. Mrs. Hunt, usually so up on teen lore, somehow didn't get the word. On the day that Alice Hunt was supposed to have gone to glory as May Day Queen, she called Alice, barely able to contain her euphoria. "Did anything interesting happen today?" Mrs. Hunt asked breathlessly. She was so giddy Alice wondered if she'd taken a nip out of the sherry. Alice honestly couldn't think of a thing—oh, yeah, except that the Cox girl from Tunica had been made May Day Queen. How boring. A deflated and devastated Mrs. Hunt decided then and there she'd have to wait for grandchildren if she wanted somebody with whom she could giggle about cute boys. Alice, unable to endure her mother's endless comments on TV news reporters' hairdos, wouldn't even watch the news with her. Daughters of ageless belles are often old before their time.

Borsch
(known in the Delta as Borscht)

*W*hat can I say, either you do or you don't. The intellectual mother, for some reason, always loves borsch—and she looks just a tad perturbed that the rest of us call it borscht.

. . .

Ingredients
1 cup shredded cabbage
1 cup chopped onions
1/2 cup shredded carrots
2 tablespoons unsalted butter
2 cups beets, shredded (julienned)
2 cups beef or chicken stock
1/2 cup reserved beet juice
Pinch of sugar
Salt and freshly ground pepper to taste
1 1/2 tablespoons fresh lemon juice
1/4 cup dry white wine
Sour cream
Fresh dill

Cook the cabbage for about ten minutes in water just to cover. Sauté the onions and carrots in the butter until wilted. Add 2 cups of the julienned beets to the onion-and-carrot mixture and mix gently. Transfer to a stockpot and add the stock plus the cabbage and cabbage water, beet juice, and sugar. Cook for 30 minutes.

Add salt, pepper, lemon juice, and wine. Correct the seasonings and continue to cook for another 15 minutes or so. Serve very hot with a dollop of sour cream and a garnish of dill, or chill thoroughly and then serve.

Don't you feel intellectual?

Serves six.

Peach Melba

*T*his is a good grande dame dessert. Yummy and fast, unlike the grande dame, but also simple and elegant—like the grande dame.

.   .   .

Ingredients
Elberta peaches (canned) or fresh peaches if available
Whiskey or cognac
1 small jar currant jelly
1 small jar apple jelly
Vanilla ice cream

In advance: Drain the juice from a can of Elberta peach halves. Combine half the juice with an equal amount of whiskey or cognac. Allow to marinate in the icebox a day or two before serving. Combine the two jellies and simmer until melted. Cool.

At serving time: Put one scoop of vanilla ice cream in each serving dish. Top with a peach half and pour melted jelly over all.

Artichoke and Oyster Soup

*A*soupçon of advice: Make this a day in advance. This is a good dish for the first course of a grande dame's dinner party. Now that we've said that, every alpha mother in the Delta will be serving Artichoke and Oyster Soup.

. . .

Ingredients

2 bunches green onions, chopped

3 garlic cloves, minced

1 stick unsalted butter

3 cans artichoke hearts, drained and quartered

3 tablespoons flour

4 cans chicken stock

1 chicken bouillon cube

1 teaspoon red pepper flakes

1 teaspoon anise seeds

1½ teaspoons salt

1 teaspoon white pepper

1 tablespoon Lea & Perrins Worcestershire Sauce

1 quart oysters, drained but juice reserved

Several dashes Tabasco

Sauté the onions and garlic in the melted butter. Add the artichokes. Sprinkle the flour over this mixture and stir to coat. Add the chicken stock and bouillon cube, red pepper, anise, salt, white pepper, and Worcestershire Sauce and simmer. In a food processor, pulse the drained oysters until barely chopped. Add the oysters and the reserved juice to the soup mixture. After about 15 minutes of cooking at a simmer, add the Tabasco.

Taste to correct seasonings but know that after refrigeration overnight the flavors will mingle and improve. Reheat to serve.

Serves six to eight as a first course.

Crabmeat Imperial

"*J*mperial" would be the operative word here. There is not a "nice" house in the Delta that doesn't have a collection of scallop shells to bake this delicious dish in. Whenever you see the shells come out, you know something special is about to happen. Now we tend to use these dishes for soap trays, etc.

.   .   .

Ingredients
1½ pounds lump crabmeat
2 tablespoons homemade mayonnaise
2 tablespoons Durkee Famous Sandwich & Salad Sauce
1 tablespoon Lea & Perrins Worcestershire Sauce
1 tablespoon small capers
Several dashes of Tabasco
Pinch of salt

Pick over the crabmeat, gently, so as not to break the lumps.

Mix the mayo, Durkee's, Lea & Perrins, capers, and Tabasco. Add a pinch of salt, too.

Pour over the crabmeat and toss gently to mix.

Place the mixture into scallop shells and top with the following:

TOPPING

> Ingredients
> *1 cup cracker crumbs*
> *Paprika*
> *3 tablespoons melted butter*

Sprinkle the cracker crumbs over the crabmeat and decorate with a splash of paprika.

Pour a little melted butter over each.

Bake for 15 to 20 minutes at 350° to 375° or until the mixture is hot and the crumbs are browned.

Serves six.

Wedding Cookies

*J*ust complicated enough for the alpha mother, who wants to practice so that Baby Girl can reel in a good catch. Not fish, but a doctor or lawyer.

. . .

Ingredients
2 sticks butter
1/2 cup confectioners' sugar, sifted, plus more for topping
2 teaspoons vanilla
1/8 teaspoon almond flavoring
2 cups sifted flour
Pinch of salt
1 cup finely chopped pecans or walnuts

Preheat oven to 325°. Cream the butter and sugar. Add the vanilla and almond flavorings.

To the flour, add a pinch of salt and the chopped nuts. Mix. Stir the flour mixture into the creamed sugar/butter. Work until blended. Shape into small balls—marble size.

Bake at 325° for 15 to 20 minutes. Roll in powdered sugar while warm. Sift extra powdered sugar over the tops.

Makes approximately five dozen cookies.

Huguenot Torte

*T*his is our friend Bland Currie's torte recipe, and it is delicious. We had a low-country brunch for Bland's niece, Alston Shackelford, for her debutante day brunch. Delicious shrimp and grits, Virginia ham and biscuits, a salad with citrus and avocado, and to top things off, this dessert—as recommended by a Charleston, South Carolina, friend who says that low-country fare is always served with a Huguenot Torte. Many in our region also have Huguenot ancestors. The motto of the Huguenot is "We will never forget." They were talking about the revocation of the Edict of Nantes, of course, not the late conflict.

·　　·　　·

Ingredients

4 eggs

3 cups sugar

8 tablespoons flour

5 teaspoons baking powder

1/2 teaspoon salt

2 cups chopped apples

2 cups chopped pecans

2 teaspoons vanilla

Whipped cream, for serving

Beat the eggs until very frothy and lemon-colored. Add the remaining ingredients in order. Pour into 2 well-buttered 8×12 inch pans. Bake at 325° for 45 minutes or until crusty brown. Scoop up with a pancake turner, keeping the crust on top. Put on a plate with whipped cream and garnish with chopped pecans.

Makes sixteen servings.

Bena's Cookies

Gayden's neighbor Patsy Thompson makes these delicious cookies, along with lots of other goodies. She is what we call a "baker." These are fast, simple, and delicious.

By the way, Patsy is also the person who bakes the delicious *and* just-the-right-size rolls for the St. James Bazaar. The ladies really don't like it when the rolls get too big. (It's a big deal to keep everything small. That's an oxymoron, which one of our friends used to define as an eight-sided idiot, but you know what it really means.) These cookies are great. You can make them any size you want!

.   .   .

Ingredients
1 cup sugar
2 sticks margarine
2 egg yolks
1½ cups flour, sifted
1 small jar strawberry jam
½ cup chopped pecans

Grease cookie sheet. Cream the sugar and margarine. Add the egg yolks and flour a little at a time until incorporated. Pat the dough onto a 17×14 inch cookie sheet. With a fork, lightly whip the jam. Spread the jam over the dough and sprinkle with pecans. Bake in a 325° to 350° oven for 15 minutes.

Cool and cut into *small* cookies.

Shrimp à la King à la Charles Wesley

The Methodist (i.e., dry) version of Chicken à la King. Methodists love chicken, and we hope they won't be upset that we revealed the secret ingredient: sherry.

. . .

Ingredients
1 can cream of mushroom soup
3/4 soup can whole milk
1 garlic clove, minced
1/2 teaspoon celery salt
1 tablespoon minced pimiento
Peeled/deveined shrimp (enough for 2 servings)
Dash or two Lea & Perrins Worcestershire Sauce
Dash or two Tabasco
Salt and white pepper to taste
2 tablespoons dry sherry

In a saucepan over medium heat, mix the mushroom soup and milk until blended. Add the garlic, celery salt, and pimiento. Add the shrimp and cook, stirring, until very hot.

Season to taste with the Worcestershire Sauce, Tabasco, salt, and pepper.

Add the sherry just before serving. This can be served in a patty shell, over toast points, or a lightly toasted English muffin half. In Louisiana, it is served in a French bread half that has been hollowed out, buttered, and toasted.

Serves two. This recipe is easily doubled.

CHAPTER VII

The Restorative Cocktail:
Toasting Our Mothers

WHEN DID YOU first realize you had turned into your mother?

Some people have senior moments—we have mother moments.

We propose a toast to those long-suffering ladies who made us what we are: replicas of themselves! When did *we* become *them*? Ruminations of this nature are best accompanied by delicious pick-ups—Tiny BLTs and Lynchburg Cheese Straws (recipes to follow) are highly appropriate—with a nice chilled white wine, or something stronger, from our beloved former bootlegger, now gone legit. And you don't even have to pretend that it's a grocery store anymore, since the county went wet officially! Nice as it is, some of our older mothers still wouldn't be caught dead inside a liquor store. That doesn't mean they are teetotalers.

"Ah hear nobody is drinking sherry anymore," Olivia Morgan Gilliam once mused. "So would you please bring me a bottle of Dubonnet?" She was sending somebody to the likker store, a place she regarded as a den of iniquity, even if it *was* pleasant to drink the sherry. Not all our sweet old dears feel that way. There was that unfortunate incident when poor old Mr. Gilliam's new bride was detained there. The elderly bridegroom drew a map of Greenville so his bride could find her way to the post office to mail her Social Security change-of-address card and she never got *past* the liquor store.

Older ladies in the Delta, Olivia Morgan excepted, prefer their drinks the color of mahogany, the stiffer the better, best if they're so potent they can get from the bar to your hand without human intervention—and we middle-aged ladies are getting there. We'll never forget when one of the younger ladies tried to persuade Caledonia Payne, the Delta Debutante Club's venerable sponsor (we don't know why that term is used—there are no commercial breaks, unless you consider it one to introduce your daughter to a banker's son), that it would be a good idea to serve only white wine and champagne at the reception. "We thought about this as a money-saving plan," said another culprit. Caledonia Payne grandly overruled this youthful folly. "Never come between an old lady and her money or her whiskey," Mrs. Payne said. You don't have to belong to a debutante club to know that old ladies in the Delta love their drinks strong.

We are reminded of one much-admired Delta lady and her regular bridge crowd—they called themselves the Little Bits. They loved bridge and played twice a week, year after year. After they finished their game (and could this be the reason they played—to have the de rigueur cocktails afterward?), some kind soul would "fix" their drinks. As if the poor "mixer" wouldn't know, they always requested a bourbon and water or Scotch and water with "just a little bit of water." One daughter-in-law says that she should have used for her mother-in-law's tombstone the immortal words "Just a little water and not much ice."

We want to go on record and say that there is one facet of our lives for which we are both grateful: having had the mothers we had. On those occasions when we have mother moments and feel that we have become them, we are grateful. Our mothers, Ann Gayden Call and Julia Morgan Hays, deserve the byline for our books. We were their stenographers. Nobody could tell a story quite like Ann Call could, and Julia Morgan wasn't half-bad either. They had the gift of framing a story and knew how to build suspense in one we'd heard many times before. The denouement was often delivered in a hushed, shocked tone, shock being the most thoroughly satisfying emotion a Delta lady experiences, as long as the one behaving shockingly is somebody else's relative.

Now that she is gone, it seems that Ann Call's mission in life was to make all of us know that we were loved. She would sit down and write us, in a beautiful hand, if she thought we were going through a hard time. We'd be hard-pressed to guess how many of us have folders of letters marked "Ann Call." They dampen our eyes, but they lift our spirits. Julia Morgan's letters were legendary in her family. She wrote her daughters long, informative and eagerly awaited letters almost daily when they were in school. After the local jet set got up to misbehaving, Julia Morgan wrote a shocked, shocked letter with the postscript "Burn this letter!" She was serious, but the letter has not been destroyed and remains one of Charlotte's most beloved treasures to this day.

Ann Call's last letter, still in a beautiful script, was to her granddaughter, Gayden Bishop Metcalfe, in London. It was filled with love and news and an admonition: Get a job because "money doesn't grow on trees." When Gayden Bishop landed a job with a famous London newspaper, we all thought, "How Ann Call would have loved this." Ann Call died in the sad spring of 2007. She always knew that even those of us who were far away loved to be kept up on Delta goings-on. To this end, she always collected the bulletins of St. James' Episcopal Church, with their notices of who was sick or had died or wed, not to mention the all-important Flowers on the Altar list from high holy days, and mailed them to us. We expect Gayden to pick up the mantle.

When Charlotte was growing up, Julia Morgan's favorite thing was going to California in the summer, to visit Charlotte's sister, Little Julia. When in California, Julia Morgan lived to have people say, "Where did you get that cute accent?" (Southern Lady Accent Rule: The farther you are from home, the thicker it gets.) Not averse to being the center of attention, she also loved being asked, "Are you from the state with the crazy governor?" Of course, that didn't narrow it down that much (and this was before the cross-dressing governor!). Though she suffered immensely through divorce, Julia Morgan always held her head high and is remembered for her valor and kindness, not to mention a deft touch with gossip.

Although we have, we hope, had some giggles about our mothers, we think it is clear that we recognize how blessed are the daughters of Southern mothers. We are glad to have their values, which today are countercultural. Our mothers taught us that a woman is not the same as a lady, and they inspired us, by example, to aspire to be ladies. It has nothing to do with money—indeed, often quite the contrary. "Lady" and "gentleman" were our mothers' highest accolades, and if that sounds old-fashioned, then more's the pity. What did they give us? An unshakable sense of self that will get us through the rough patches, no matter how difficult things may become. We'll always be able to say to ourselves, when we think we can't make it another minute, when we feel we have been humiliated: "Get out there and curtsey. Hold your head high. Reply in kind." And our personal favorite: "I told you so." These are the adages that carry us through life.

She always said that one day we would thank her—and, as usual, Mother was right.

RECIPES FOR TOASTING
OUR MOTHERS

WHEN YOU sit down to toast your Southern mother, you'll need the proper pick-ups. Mama wouldn't want you to settle for potato chips (unless, of course, you consider putting them in a casserole).

We have a lot of cheese dishes—and that would suit our mothers just fine.

The critic and editor Clifton Fadiman once described cheese as "man's leap toward immortality." Certainly, he was talking about cream cheese and the South. Cream cheese has been put in everything, including (and especially) grits. Cheese makes the most humble dish smooth and tasty.

In the South, gourmets were born overnight by their creative dealings with cream cheese. Now cream cheese means something like brie at room temp. In our mothers' and grandmothers' day, the operative words were "melba rounds" or "toast points." If things were really going to be fancy, we had canapés.

We learned about cream cheese through our mothers. At breakfast, it was orange marmalade and ginger in cream cheese to spread on banana nut bread. Cream cheese was their favorite for afternoon and cocktail fare, too.

After our mothers had spread as much cream cheese as they could, and they had depleted the Wheat Thin/melba round supply in the Delta, they started to stuff. Same cheese—just no spreader. They attacked celery stalks and cherry tomatoes with a vengeance, and we must say it was a blessed relief for the cracker market. Somewhere along the way, pesto and sun-dried tomatoes came into vogue—new spread materials. Now we are into bruschetta and tapas. Goodness.

Lynchburg Cheese Straws

*T*his is a recipe from Jessica Bemis Ward's *Food to Die For,* honoring the Old City Cemetery in Lynchburg, Virginia. It's hard to have drinks in the Delta without cheese straws, and so we decided to introduce our Delta friends to this scrumptious Virginia version. Jessica says that you can vary the ingredients a bit according to your own preferences. And, best of all, nobody has to die for us to enjoy them (though, along with tomato aspic with home-made mayonnaise, they are the ultimate funeral food).

.　　　.　　　.

Ingredients
*1 brick (10 ounces) Cracker Barrel Extra Sharp
    Cheddar cheese, grated*
1 cup butter
2 1/2 cups sifted flour
1 teaspoon salt
1 teaspoon cayenne pepper

Cream the room-temperature cheese using a mixer. Scrape down the sides of the mixer. Add the room-temperature butter, and cream 10 minutes.

If possible, for added flavor, let this mixture set overnight in the refrigerator. Add the flour, salt, and pepper, and cream well. Form into strips, using disks with serrated spacing. Bake in a 350° degree oven for 10 minutes or until blushed.

Tiny BLTs

When Ann Call was older, had broken her hip, and was nearly blind, she knew that Gayden worried about her. She would fix her drink, take it to bed, lie down, and telephone Gayden to say she was in bed and safe—and prepared to enjoy her nightly libation. Ann Call wasn't going to fall or miss her evening toddy. And she loved tiny finger sandwiches—a perfect accompaniment for an evening toddy.

Our friend Robert St. John has a wonderful recipe for tiny tomato sandwiches—so perfect, in fact, that Robert's rendition was used for the tomato sandwiches served on a silver tray at the reception after Ann Call's funeral. Robert's recipe includes hot bacon grease in the (homemade!) mayonnaise.

We love tiny treats to accompany our sometimes not-so-tiny cocktails. These Tiny BLTs are served on a regular basis at the morning meetings of the garden club and then, later in the evening, recycled for the cocktail hour. Or do we mean hours?

Ingredients
1 loaf sliced white bread
1 cup mayonnaise
1/2 stick butter, melted
1/2 teaspoon salt
1/2 teaspoon black pepper
1 teaspoon paprika
3 tablespoons parsley flakes
1 package (3 ounces) crumbled bacon
12 to 15 cherry or Roma tomatoes in 1/4-inch slices

Using a small round cutter that is slightly larger than the tomato slices, cut the bread into 50 circles. Toast on cookie sheet for 30 minutes at 250°. Mix together all the other ingredients, except the bacon and tomatoes. Chill several hours.

Spread the mixture on the bread rounds and top each with a slice of tomato. Sprinkle with bacon. Arrange on tray or bed of bean sprouts.

Serves fifty. Not suitable for freezing.

Salami Stack-ups

*T*hese are the kinds of things created by our pre-Viking mothers—that is, before the renaissance of gourmet cooking in Greenwood, Mississippi, the home of the Viking Range Corporation. Fred Carl invented the gourmet range trying to come up with something perfect for his wife, Margaret. We're glad he did—it's been a boon to Greenwood, the Delta, and cooks everywhere.

But we still like salami stack-ups.

.   .   .

Ingredients
8 ounces cream cheese
Lea & Perrins Worcestershire Sauce
Horseradish (from the cooler section, not fresh)
Dash Tabasco
Sliced cocktail salami

Mash/mix the cream cheese with the Worcestershire Sauce, horseradish, and a dash of Tabasco.

Spread the tops of four rounds of salami with the cream cheese mixture. Stack and ice (as in frosting a cake) the entire outside. Chill.

When ready to serve, slice into small wedges.

One designer recipe says that statistics have proven that one 8-ounce package of cream cheese will ice three 8-ounce packages of salami (pre-sliced).

Makes approximately four dozen.

Curried Chicken Balls

A nother great treat for those late afternoons when we gather with our friends to deliberate on those existential questions. These amounts are approximate. You must add enough mayonnaise or chutney to suit your taste. We prefer a bit more curry powder and chutney.

.　　.　　.

Ingredients

1/2 pound Philadelphia Cream Cheese

3 tablespoons homemade mayonnaise

1 cup chopped cooked chicken breast

1 1/2 tablespoons curry powder

1 tablespoon chopped chutney

   (Major Grey used to be the only choice down here,

   but go for the best you can find.)

1/2 teaspoon salt

1 cup coarsely chopped slivered almonds

3/4 cup grated coconut

Allow the cream cheese to soften at room temperature. Combine the mayonnaise, chicken, curry, chutney, salt, and almonds.

Fold into the cream cheese and mix well. Be sure to add just enough mayo and chutney to bind your mixture. Taste and correct the seasonings. Roll into small balls and then roll to coat in coconut. Cover tightly and refrigerate.

Makes approximately thirty-six bites.

Chutney Cream Cheese Mold

Ingredients
2 packages (¹/₂ pound each) cream cheese, softened
2 cups sharp grated Cheddar cheese
6 tablespoons sherry or white wine
1 teaspoon curry powder
2 tablespoons Lea & Perrins Worcestershire Sauce
¹/₂ teaspoon salt
Chutney
Ground peanuts
Chopped green onions
Coconut, shredded

Mix cream cheese, Cheddar cheese, sherry, curry powder, Worcestershire Sauce, and salt. Press into an 8- or 9-inch round cake pan that has been lined with Saran Wrap. Chill. This can be done days ahead.

When ready to serve, unmold on a flat tray. Spoon chutney over the top, followed by ground peanuts, chopped green onions, and coconut. Serve with Wheat Thins.

Holiday Cheese Balls—
Good for Cocktails, Too

*C*an we have a holiday without a cheese ball? The answer is no!

Holiday cheese balls start appearing the first of December and continue right through the New Year. Our icebox looks like cold storage for the bowling alley. This is one of our favorite recipes.

·　　·　　·

Ingredients
1 pound soft buttery blue cheese such as Gorgonzola
2 packages (3 ounces each) Philadelphia Cream Cheese
3 ounces brandy
Chopped walnuts

Allow the cheeses to soften at room temperature. Mix together and add the brandy. Be sure to blend well. Shape into a ball and coat with the nuts. Cover well and refrigerate overnight before serving.

Serves three to four dozen.

Patty Jones's Chicken Liver Pate

 atty Jones isn't a real person—that was a nickname for our dear friend the late Josie Pattison Wynn, who was about as far from being a Patty as you could be. Jones was her mother's maiden name. We teasingly call this Patty Jones Chicken Liver Pate, as we teasingly called Josie Patty Jones. A great cook, Josie was a purist at heart. But her pate is definitely more Delta than Paris.

. . .

Ingredients

1 pound chicken livers

¾ cup sliced mushrooms

¼ cup chopped green onions

2 sticks unsalted butter

¼ cup cognac

1 teaspoon salt

⅛ teaspoon freshly ground black pepper

⅛ teaspoon cayenne pepper

¼ teaspoon allspice

⅛ teaspoon thyme

Chopped parsley

Sliced mushrooms for garnish

Wash, dry, and chop the livers.

Sauté the mushrooms and onions in the butter for about 5 minutes, remove with a slotted spoon, and set aside.

Add the livers to the pan, stir, and cook until done (about 5 minutes).

Put the livers into a food processor, add the mushrooms, cognac, and seasonings. Process briefly. If the mixture is too thick, add a little melted butter.

Pack in crocks or a mold and chill.

Unmold. Decorate with parsley and mushrooms. Serve at room temperature.

Cocktail Casserole

*H*ere is proof that there are Methodists who partake. Only a Methodist could serve a casserole with cocktails. But, in true Methodist tradition, this is delicious.

When Mother sent us to the grocery for crabmeat (canned, that is), she always said, "Geisha, flaked." This recipe is good for canned crabmeat, and it doesn't have to be flaked or Geisha.

•   •   •

1 can (6 ounces) crabmeat
1 package (8 ounces) Philadelphia Ceam Cheese
1 tablespoon whole milk
3 teaspoons finely minced green onions
1 teaspoon horseradish
1/2 teaspoon white pepper
1/4 teaspoon salt
1 teaspoon Lea & Perrins Worcestershire Sauce
1/2 cup sliced almonds

Drain the crabmeat.

Allow the cream cheese to soften and mash with a fork. Add all the remaining ingredients except the almonds.

Spread in an ovenproof dish and top with the almonds. Bake at 375° for at least 15 minutes or until good and hot. Serve with melba rounds.

Serves six to eight with cocktails.

Basic Spreads for the Cocktail Hour

*E*very afternoon at around five o'clock, Orlando Crittenden, a much-loved cousin and dear friend, dropped in to visit Julia Morgan's father. A non-cook, Julia Morgan felt like Julia Child when she spread crackers (Ritz, we seem to remember) with cream cheese and chives for them. Alas, her way with the Ritz cracker is lost to posterity, but here are some very tasty spreads.

.   .   .

Ingredients
2 packages (8 ounces each) Philadelphia Cream Cheese
1/2 cup cream
1/4 small onion, grated
Lea & Perrins Worcestershire Sauce, Tabasco, and salt to taste

Soften the cream cheese and add enough of the cream to make the mixture spreadable. Stir in the grated onion, and flavor to taste.

Use homemade mayonnaise in place of the cream if you like, or use half cream and half mayo.

Spread bread of your choice (crust removed, so your mother won't come back to haunt you) with the cream cheese mixture.

Decorate with sliced green olives, pimiento strips, anchovies, shrimp, or just parsley.

You can get creative and roll the bread (with your filling of choice, even adding a gherkin pickle), chill, and slice, making pinwheels.

To the basic spread add capers and a little caper juice and top with a piece of smoked salmon. Serve with a tiny lemon wedge.

Instead of bread, spread thin slices of ham with guava jelly or pepper jelly. Spread the cream cheese mixture over the ham slices and roll. Chill and slice into bite-size pieces.

The possibilities are endless—just remember to *always* remove the crusts from your bread. Mama would not be pleased if she thought she'd raised the kind of daughter who leaves crust on a finger sandwich. Can we say this too often? Are we becoming harpies like our mothers?

Chipped Beef and Cream Cheese
à la Cora Louise

*T*his recipe comes from late Cora Louise McGee Belford, who grew up in Leland, Mississippi, but lived much of her adult life in New York City, where her husband, Lee Belford, was an Episcopal minister and college professor. She returned to Leland, to live on Deer Creek (the very same gracious street where her relative Ann Call lived as a girl). By then retired, Lee Belford became a mainstay, always willing to take services at St. James and at St. John's in Leland. Cora Louise was descended from a governor of the state (but not one of the crazy ones!). She and Lee Belford became one of the most loved couples in Leland and Greenville.

Cora Louise would double and often triple this recipe and serve it in a chafing dish. Having had the NYC stay, she served this with rye crisp toast points.

Not having had the NYC experience, Gayden serves hers in the au gratin dish with whatever she is lucky enough to find . . . usually melba rounds.

. . .

Ingredients
½ cup chopped pecans, not too small
3 tablespoons unsalted butter
½ teaspoon salt
½ cup minced green pepper
1 small onion, grated
1 jar (2.5 ounces) dried beef, chopped rather small
11 ounces Philadelphia Cream Cheese, softened at room temperature
1 cup sour cream
White pepper, a good sprinkling
Dash or two Tabasco
Milk, if needed

In two tablespoons of the butter, toast the pecans in a slow oven until lightly browned. Salt.

In the remaining 1 tablespoon butter, lightly sauté the green pepper and onion. Add the chopped beef to the above mixture and stir until the beef is incorporated—just a stir or two.

Add the cream cheese and sour cream, stirring lightly to mix. Add half the toasted nuts.

Season with a sprinkling of white pepper and a dash or two of Tabasco. Top with the remaining nuts.

Using an au gratin dish that will hold 3 cups, bake for 20 minutes at 350°. If necessary, thin to desired consistency with whole milk.

Serves ten.

Salted Pecans

$\mathcal{N}$o Southern mother worth her—ahem—salt lacks a recipe for salted pecans. We use them for lunches, receptions, and evening affairs where drinks are being served. This recipe comes from Charlotte's cousin the late Nancy Smythe, who got it from her mother, Mayree Smythe.

Far be it from us to amend Mayree's recipe, but some of us use a half stick of margarine instead of a whole stick! Butter will burn too fast, thus the oleo (as she called it).

.　　.　　.

Ingredients
2 1/2 cups pecan halves
Salt
1/2 stick margarine

Rinse the pecans in cold water. Drain.

Put the wet pecans in a shallow, flat pan (jelly roll pan/cookie sheet with sides), salt, and roast at 300° for about 10 minutes, then turn and roast another 10 minutes or just until dry.

Put margarine pats over the pecans, return to the oven, and

roast another 10 minutes. Turn with a spatula, mixing well, and roast until golden brown, approximately 10 more minutes. Be careful because when these begin to brown they do so quickly. Turn out on a brown paper bag to cool.

A variation on the theme:

Wet the pecans with cold water and place in one layer on a jelly roll pan.

Pour on Worcestershire sauce (Lea & Perrins) and toss until the nuts are well coated. Sprinkle with salt.

Roast in a 300° oven, turning about every ten minutes, until the nuts are golden brown and toasted dry.

INDEX